ARCHITECTS' GRAVESITES

ARCHITECTS' GRAVESITES

A SERENDIPITOUS GUIDE

HENRY H. KUEHN

Foreword by Barry Bergdoll and Afterword by Paul Goldberger

The MIT Press | Cambridge, Massachusetts | London, England

© 2017 Massachusetts Institute
of Technology

All rights reserved. No part of this book may be reproduced in any form by any electronic or mechanical means (including photocopying, recording, or information storage and retrieval) without permission in writing from the publisher.

This book was set in Odile by The MIT Press.

Printed and bound in the United States of America.

Library of Congress
Cataloging-in-Publication Data

Names: Kuehn, Henry H., author.
Title: Architects' gravesites : a serendipitous guide / Henry H. Kuehn.
Description: Cambridge, MA : The MIT Press, 2017.
Identifiers: LCCN 2016037855 | ISBN 9780262533478 (pbk. : alk. paper)
Subjects: LCSH: Architects—United States—Biography. |
  Architects—Tombs—United States—Guidebooks. | Sepulchral
  monuments—United States—Guidebooks.
Classification: LCC NA736 .K84 2017 | DDC 720.92/2 [B]—dc23 LC record available at https://lccn.loc.gov/2016037855

10 9 8 7 6 5 4 3 2 1

To two good friends who wish to remain anonymous. Without their initiation of the project, their research, and their unflagging support, this book would not exist.

CONTENTS

Foreword by Barry Bergdoll ix
Preface xiii
Acknowledgments xvii

Architects' Gravesites 1

Geographical Groupings 121
Afterword by Paul Goldberger 129

FOREWORD

Lector, si monumentum requiris circumspice ("Reader, if you seek his monument look around you") is the sole marker of Sir Christopher Wren's (died 1723) tomb in London's St. Paul's Cathedral. Unadorned by either a portrait or memorial of any kind, this inscription, set below the dome of the most monumental of Wren's many church designs, raises the question of the best way in which architects—who devoted their lives, for the most part, to conceiving monuments that might out-last them, and it is hoped many generations to come—might themselves enter into both eternity and memory. A similar sentiment is evoked in a granite plaque set in the herringbone brick paving on the plaza at the center of the Columbia University campus, one of the great designs of Charles Follen McKim, admired by many, few of whom pay attention to the inscription below their feet as they take in one of the grandest public spaces in New York, although McKim was laid to rest far from any of his great civic designs, which transformed the face of New York in the years on either side of 1900. As we learn in this marvelous bio-gazetteer of American architectural death assembled as an act of homage and curiosity by Henry Kuehn, McKim also enjoys a lasting memorial mention where he is buried, surrounded by his family in a cemetery in Orange, New Jersey. Public figure or private individual, civic artist or simple citizen, the architect's public and private personae come definitively to the fore in the place, shape, and form of the final resting place.

Final wishes are, of course, always subject to the decisions made by those who survive—family, fellow artists— as to how to mark the final resting place of architects. How many designers leave behind instructions, or even a design destined to be posthumous in its execution, for the act or object that will mark their final resting place, or record the scattering of their ashes over a treasured or significant landscape? At least as early as the Renaissance the notion that great architects deserved honors in the public realm, sometimes on or in the very monuments they created, emerged, a practice that grew exponentially with the rise of the cult of the civic hero in the Age of the Enlightenment, and in the wake of the American and French Revolutions. Ironically enough, for instance, when the great French eighteenth-century architect Jacques-Germain Soufflot was given a grave in the crypt of the French Pantheon, one of the great catalysts of the rituals of the memorialization of secular heroes as public exemplar, it was on the basis of a promise made by his original clients, the monks of the Abbey of Ste. Genevieve to allow him alone burial among them in the great church of Ste. Genevieve, still under construction when Soufflot died in 1780. Soufflot's great monumental church dedicated to the patron saint of Paris, had been converted in 1791 under the French Revolution into a temple to honor *grands hommes* (great men). Renamed the Pantheon, the building would host the remains of Voltaire, Rousseau, and countless other philosophers, men of state, scientists, over the decades, but would in fact never house an architect other than its original author, who could never expect that he would have created, or come to eternal rest in, one of the grandest civic monuments of nineteenth century France.

With the rise of public cemeteries, divorced from churchyards, in early nineteenth-century Europe and North America, the conflation of public commemoration and private memorial became common, particularly for figures—architects among them— who had obtained a great public persona during their lifetime. The great cemeteries of London, Paris, and later Munich, Berlin, Rome, Genoa, St. Petersburg, and other cities with picturesque cemeteries are filled with monuments to architects, often designed by another architect designated by the deceased's colleagues to embody the essence of his or her contribution to architecture. Here the paradoxical charge arises to design something in the style of the deceased, if no instructions have been left behind, a type recorded here in the tomb Tallmadge designed for Louis Sullivan. So for instance Félix Duban designed, in the St. Charles cemetery in Marseille, a tomb for Michel-Robert Penchaud (1772-1833), author of some of the most severe neoclassical monuments of Marseille, in a chaste neoclassical form, inscribed with the ground plans and elevations of some of Penchaud's civic monuments, even though Duban's entire career was based on a rebellion from neoclassical orthodoxy. Few are the architects, like Percier and Fontaine in Paris, Schinkel in Berlin, or Ralph Rapson, whose tomb is included here, who have the foresight to design their own tomb, and the good fortune for their admirers to see it executed as designed. Even rarer is the architect who is interred and memorialized, not in a churchyard or cemetery, but in one of the finest buildings he or she might have designed; Bertram Goodhue and William Strickland are the examples found in Kuehn's treasure hunt. Here the gamble for eternity is doubled, for the architects who almost always build with the hope that buildings will outlast them, here have their own concrete memory on earth tied to the future fate of their architectural creations, entrusted not to the promise of perpetual maintenance often honored only in the breach in cemeteries but rather to the modern legislation of historic preservation to keep a building safe from future alteration or real estate pressures.

Although architects enjoy the honors of the Hall of Fame of Great Americans at the former New York University campus in the Bronx, there is no single pantheon for the burial of America's great designers of buildings. But as Henry Kuehn has shown us, Graceland Cemetery in Chicago is as close as one can get to a Valhalla for the great figures of Chicago, a city like no other associated with its contributions to American architectural history. And here it is clear that the professional ethos of Chicago's architects, has made Graceland into one of the richest landscapes of architectural honors anywhere in the country. This book is a delightful journey into the last bids for memory granted to designers whose work has transformed the face of American cities.

Barry Bergdoll

Professor of Art History and Archeology
Columbia University
New York, New York

Former Philip Johnson Curator of
Architecture & Design
Museum of Modern Art
New York, New York

PREFACE

My interest in this project probably goes all the way back to a course in architectural history that I took from the renowned Vincent Scully. Despite having a career in business, I was profoundly influenced by the Scully course, which led me to several architecture-related endeavors during the ensuing years. These included affiliations with the Society of Architectural Historians, the Graham Foundation for Advanced Studies in the Fine Arts, the Architecture and Design Committee of the Art Institute of Chicago, and the Chicago Architecture Foundation. It was as a director of the Graceland Cemetery tour of the Chicago Architecture Foundation that I came to realize that Graceland is the final resting place for a significant number of prominent American architects.

Thus began my task of researching, visiting, and photographing sites across the country. In this quest I identified over 200 architects of interest and located the gravesites for most of these.

As I dug into this project, the fundamental question that arose was: how have the men and women who designed the country's most important and impactful architecture been remembered? Architects from the beginning of civilization have created incredible monuments—the Great Pyramids of Giza and the Parthenon come to mind. In America, architects have created impactful monuments such as the Lincoln Memorial and the St. Louis Arch. Having the interest in and capability of designing such lasting edifices, it seemed logical that these important architects would have put some thought and effort into how they themselves would be remembered.

I was surprised by the results. Certainly a few of the architects I investigated have the imposing and self-congratulatory memorials that I had imagined would exist. However, very few have monuments that in any way depict the architectural style for which the architect is noted. Instead, many are situated inconspicuously in lovely, serene, and out-of-the-way settings. The cremated remains of some of these great designers reside in highly unlikely places—the closet of a daughter, or the attic of a house once designed and lived in by the architect. For most of these architects the monuments are quite simple and understated—often just a headstone noting simply their names and dates and, occasionally, that this person had been an architect. It seems strange that these great architects, who created landmark structures during their lives, put so little thought into how they would be memorialized for time eternal. Apparently most of these architectural giants, like most of us ordinary people, either did not feel like dealing with death or felt that a lasting memorial for them was not important. What sets this group apart, perhaps, is that, in a striking number of cases, they chose not to have a marker at all but instead directed that their ashes be scattered at a place of special importance to them.

One can only hope that current and future architects will be inspired by their peers and, thereby, revive the diverse art of grave marker design. If this opportunity is ignored, the final places of today's important architects will go largely unnoticed by future generations.

When it came time to put pen to paper I needed to establish ground rules for this effort. Since tomes have been written about most of these architects, and ample information about their works and careers can be found elsewhere, I have chosen not to provide lengthy biographical information. Rather, I concentrate on their gravesites and share the information I have found regarding how their monuments came to be.

Deciding who among all the architects of the world is notable and American was a challenge that required setting some limits. As a result there are probably a number of architects and designers who the reader feels should have been included but were not. I have included a number of architects who are not American but did significant work and were highly influential in this country—and, I might add, they have some wonderful graves! I also have included some landscape designers who worked closely with major architects on significant projects. Finally, I have included several engineers who are responsible for designing structures that have had enormous impact on our country.

It is no surprise that the highest honor that the American Institute of Architects awards in its field, the AIA Gold Medal, has been bestowed upon forty-two of the architects included in this project. What is interesting is that many were given the awards long after their death, meaning that their influence had not been realized until many years after they had passed.

ACKNOWLEDGMENTS

In taking on this endeavor I was the recipient of valuable assistance from many people. I want to give special thanks to Susan Johnson Robbins, who helped immeasurably with the graphic design ideas that shaped this book from the very start. Pauline Saliga at the Society of Architectural Historians put me in touch with many experts on specific architects.

Most of the photographs in this book were taken by Henry Kuehn. Several were taken by others and their names are listed within the following acknowledgments. There were a limited number where I was not able to identify the photographer but I will be happy to do so in subsequent editions if photographers contact me.

Aiding in the research and in procuring photos were: Una Abraham, Robert Adlet, The Arcosanti Organization, B. B. Archer, Anna Artis, Eleanor Bacon, John Barley, Carol Ross Barney, Betty Blum, Melanie Boubreau,

Diane MacLean Boumenot, Barbara Callas, Robert Campbell, Canadian Architectural Museum, Alejandrina Catalano, Michael Churchill, Coleman Coker, Jill Cook, Michael Core, Esther Danner, Carlos Davidson, John Davis, Robert DeBlois, Jennifer Dominquez, Doug Dworsky, Pepita Ehrnrooth-Jokinen, Joan R. Francis, Laura Gallery, Jim Garrison, Tim Garrity, Barbara Gossett, George Granberry, Chandra Goldsmith Gray, Frank Harmon, Carol Harper, Adrian Harris, Bente Hartmann, Renata Hejduk, Steven Hillyer, Harma Holiday, Augusta Holland, Caryl Horn, Tim Horning, Mia Hyseli, Neil Jackson, Frank Jackson, Mary Jones, Michael Jones, Linda Kinsey, Hanne Sue Kirsch, Faith Koons, Phyllis Lambert, Kristin Larsen, Joanne Lawson, Michael Leach, James Logan, Ann Lumsden, Alexandra Lescaze, Victor Legorreta, Carolyn Loughlin, Geoffrey Lloyd, James Logan, Suzanne Maicke, Gayle MacGregor, Elizabeth Manny, Margo Warnecke Merck, Michigan Modern Wordpress, Jason Miller, Jacquelyn Mockbee, Michael Moran, Kim Moretti, Jeanne Moutoussamy-Ashe, James Neal, Dion Neutra, Raymond Neutra, Terry Nielson, Richard Olson, Nancy Orocio, Chistina Parachiv, Diane Payne, Brigitte Peterhans, Stephen Pinkerton, Patrick Rafferty, Delores Robles-Martinez, Tim Rice, Andy Rider, James Ryan, Jeffery Sample, Celia Scott, Melvin Sellers, Sue Sellers, Louis Skidmore, Jr., Linda Smith, Wayne Somers, Lynette Spitz, Sara Super, Arthur Takeuchi, Mary Alice Jervay Thatch, Melissa Traub, Paul Turner, Jose Urrea, Craig Walkapich, Pat Welsh, Ann Wheelock, Stan Winship, Paul Williams, Michael Woo, the Woodlands Historical Mansion, and Aleksandra Woods.

Further assisting me with information or photographs were: Nicholas Adams, Jesseca Baumert, Julie Humphrey Belew, Barry Bergdoll, Zac Brownson, Billy Carew, Gladys Dinkeloo, Dayle Dooley, Melinda Garcia, Josh Hartmann, Richard Homan, Patrick Kavanagh, Aaron Kiley, Eric Kozen, Theresa Labianca, Bill Lucas, Mike Lynch, Peter McMann, Fred Noyes, Lynn Osmond, John Papa, Beth Savastana, Maria Scileppi, Dave and Nancy Selander, Jonathan Self, Alan Strauber, Donald Strum, John Tschirch, Margot Weller, and Meg Winslow. The Mount Auburn Cemetery Historical Collections was also extremely helpful and supportive throughout this project. No doubt there are others who contributed to this effort that have been forgotten by me over the years that it has taken to see the project to fruition. I regret any such omissions.

On a personal note, I am delighted that my ten-year-old grandson, Hank Peace, after accompanying me on several cemetery explorations, has experienced the excitement of finding treasure in these wonderful places.

Finally, I want to thank my wife Marti for her encouragement and for keeping me on course for these many years.

ARCHITECTS' GRAVESITES

Alvar AALTO
(1898-1976)

Hietaniemi Cemetery,
Helsinki, Finland

❁ AIA Gold Medal 1963

It may seem strange to begin the list of architects with one who is not generally considered an American architect. However, Aalto designed two buildings in America that received much attention. His acclaimed Finnish Pavilion at the 1939 New York World's Fair led to a professorship for him at MIT. While there he designed the much-admired Baker House, a large serpentine dormitory that overlooks the Charles River in Cambridge, Massachusetts. Ironically, the namesake of this building, Dean Everett Moore Baker, died in the same plane crash in Egypt that took the life of architect Matthew Nowicki, who will be discussed later.

His second wife, Elissa, also an architect, designed Aalto's grave marker.

Julian Francis ABELE
(1881-1950)

Eden Cemetery,
Collingdale, Pennsylvania

In 1902, Abele was the first African American to earn a degree in architecture from the University of Pennsylvania. He spent most of his career with Horace Trumbauer's prestigious firm in Philadelphia, where he had a significant role in the design of the Philadelphia Museum of Art and the Widener Library in Cambridge, Massachusetts. Trumbauer recognized Abele's talent and supported his extensive travels in Europe and his attendance at the Ecole des Beaux-Arts in Paris.

Upon Trumbauer's death, Abele became head of the firm and went on to design several buildings for Duke University, including the chapel and the administration building. At the time he received these commissions, Duke did not accept black students and Abele was not permitted to stay on campus during his frequent visits there.

Abele's grave is marked with a tablet bearing his name and dates. As a final tribute, Duke University's main quadrangle now bears his name.

Raimund ABRAHAM
(1933-2010)

Mazunte, Mexico

Though Abraham was born and trained in Austria, he had significant impact on the American architectural community by his being part of the visionary faculty created by John Hejduk at Cooper Union in New York City. His enigmatic, poetic drawings, several about a visionary "house,"

were a major influence on a generation of students. Yet he was also a practical builder. His best-known work is the Austrian Cultural Forum in New York City, which received high praise from critic Kenneth Frampton.

Abraham is buried near the home he designed for himself in Mazunte, Mexico. His grave marker is a "house" of bricks built by his friend and neighbor, Checo Diaz. His ashes are in an urn buried beneath the marker. The flower urn atop the marker was purchased years earlier by Abraham and his daughter.

Dankmar ADLER
(1844-1900)

Mt. Mayriv Cemetery, Chicago, Illinois

Adler was a partner with the great architect Louis Sullivan in the firm of Adler & Sullivan. Having already established his architectural firm, Adler recognized the brilliance of the young Sullivan and made him a partner at the age of twenty-seven. Adler's business acumen and engineering skills melded nicely with Sullivan's architectural design talents and led to the firm's impressive success. Frank Lloyd Wright was also hired into the firm during this time. At the turn of the century, Adler parted company with Sullivan as a result of the lack of business caused by a poor national economy. Adler left architecture and, in what seems an ignominious step backward, became a salesman for an elevator company for a short time prior to his death.

Adler's mother died giving birth to him in Germany. Thus, he was given the ominous name of Dankmar (meaning "bitter thanks") by his father. He and his father immigrated to the United States when Adler was ten. He is buried in his family's plot with a panel of the family's marker dedicated to Adler with the inscription: "Faithful in every relationship in life, true to himself and his god, the world is better for his having lived."

The family monument is capped with a great column taken from Chicago's Central Music Hall, a building Adler had designed and which was torn down the same year as his death. This is a unique example of an architect being commemorated with an actual artifact from one of his works.

David ADLER
(1883-1949)

Graceland Cemetery, Chicago, Illinois

Another Adler, no relation to Dankmar Adler, was David Adler, who designed over 200 buildings. These primarily were large residences for wealthy clients in the Chicago area. Adler was educated at Princeton and began working as an architect in 1911, eventually forming his own firm. Years later, when his firm had become quite large, he realized the need to become registered and begrudgingly took the state licensing exam. He failed on his first attempt; in some of his answers he stated that he wasn't involved in such things since he had people in his office who did them for him! He ultimately was licensed in 1929.

His grave is located within the family plot of his wife's prominent family, the Keiths. Rather than suggesting anything of his own importance as an architect, his marker fits in quietly among similar gravestones of other Keith family members.

Gregory AIN
(1908-1988)

Pacific Ocean

Ain became interested in architecture after visiting the Schindler House in southern California as a youth. He studied architecture at the University of Southern California but dropped out after two years because he felt the curriculum there was too committed to Beaux-Arts style.

He worked for Richard Neutra for five years before heading off on his own to design "common architecture for common people." Ain created a number of modest modernist houses in southern California before completing his career as dean of the school of architecture at the University of Pennsylvania.

After his death, his ashes were cast upon the Pacific Ocean.

Chester Holmes ALDRICH
(1871-1940)

Italy

Aldrich attended Columbia University in New York City before studying at the Ecole des Beaux-Arts in Paris. His early work was with the firm of Carrere & Hastings, where he produced the firm's competition drawings for the New York Public Library. In 1903, he left Carrere & Hastings to establish a firm with William Adams Delano. The firm of Delano & Aldrich became known for several important Beaux-Arts projects that they designed for such prominent clients as the Rockefellers, Astors, and Whitneys.

In 1935, Aldrich left Delano & Aldrich to head the American Academy in Rome, a city for which he had a lifelong love. It was there he died and is believed to be buried.

Peirce ANDERSON
(1870-1924)

Graceland Cemetery,
Chicago, Illinois

Anderson was a partner in the prolific Chicago-based firm of Graham, Anderson, Probst & White, which designed office buildings and commercial structures throughout the country. Anderson was trained at the Ecole des Beaux-Arts in Paris, and this influence can be seen in the classically derived buildings that GAP&W designed during his time at the firm, such as Chicago's Union Station.

Fittingly, Anderson's monument, designed by the GAP&W office, is an enormous classical sarcophagus, surrounded by a colonnade. His coffin was lowered by crane into the aboveground burial chamber. The only indication of Anderson's identity on the monument is a small cameo affixed to one side bearing Anderson's profile and name.

Charles Bowler ATWOOD
(1849-1895)

Millbury Central Cemetery,
Millbury, Massachusetts

After attending Harvard, Atwood worked for William Ware's Boston architectural firm. It was Ware who recommended Atwood to Daniel Burnham, who was looking for a senior design architect after the sudden death in 1891 of his partner, John Wellborn Root. Atwood soon became a trusted designer for Burnham and assumed the role of Architect in Chief at the Columbian Exposition in Chicago. It was there that he designed the building for which he is most remembered, the Fine Arts Building, which was later transformed into the Museum of Science and Industry.

Despite his gifts as a designer, Atwood was mysterious and aloof and was often absent from Burnham's firm for long periods. He seemed constantly in poor health. Because of his unpredictable behavior, Burnham eventually dismissed him. Atwood died just nine days later.

After his death, several surprises came to light. It was discovered that Atwood was an opium addict. Also, a woman emerged who claimed to be his wife, something that shocked all of his Chicago associates, including Burnham, who thought Atwood was single. Eventually, the courts honored the marriage, and the woman, Marian Singer, became heir to his assets. Atwood is buried beneath a large granite monument capped with a cross.

Henry AUSTIN
(1804-1891)

Grove Street Cemetery,
New Haven, Connecticut

Austin was an early and prolific architect who created many works throughout New England. His stone marker bears his and his wife's names and indicates as well the tragedy that befell his family with the deaths of three children at the ages of two months, two years, and eleven years. His epitaph reads: "A good designer and a sound builder."

Edmund BACON
(1910-2005)

Phoenixville, Pennsylvania

After studying architecture at Cornell University, Bacon continued on at the Cranbrook Academy with Eliel Saarinen. From there he returned to his native Philadelphia, where he eventually became director of the city planning commission and had a major role in implementing a new city master plan.

Bacon was cremated and his ashes were scattered on the grounds of a favorite family retreat built by his mother in Phoenixville, Pennsylvania.

are the names of Bacon and his wife as well as the attribution of his having designed the Lincoln Memorial.

Henry BACON
(1866-1924)

Oakdale Cemetery,
Wilmington, North Carolina

❊ AIA Gold Medal 1923

Bacon was a Beaux-Arts architect who, as a young designer, worked for McKim, Mead & White. Late in his career he received the commission for his best-known work, the Lincoln Memorial in Washington, D.C.

His own monument is a tall stone tablet embellished with a flourish of stylized wheat. Embossed on the tablet

Edward Larrabee BARNES
(1915-2004)

Brookside Cemetery,
Mount Desert, Maine

❊ AIA Gold Medal 2007

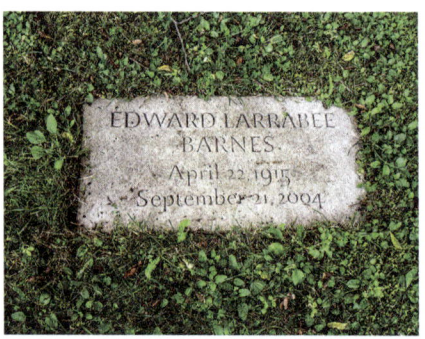

Born in Chicago, Barnes went to Harvard as an undergraduate and then studied under Walter Gropius and Marcel Breuer at the Harvard Graduate School of Design. His prolific career included the design of housing projects, office buildings, and museums. He was awarded the highest honor of the American Institute of Architects, the Gold Medal, three years after his death.

His remains reside among those of other family members in a remote island cemetery along the rugged coast of Maine. His site is marked with a simple stone bearing his name and dates.

George BARNETT
(1815-1898)

Bellefontaine Cemetery,
St. Louis, Missouri

Barnett was known at the "dean of St. Louis architecture" for his many buildings and his influence on fellow architects in that city. One of his most noted works is the Old Courthouse in St. Louis.

He is buried in a family plot alongside his wife and a daughter, Nancy. His grave was unmarked until 1965, when the Barnett family provided a red granite tablet inscribed with his and his wife's names.

Edward Charles BASSETT
(1922-1999)

Bassett was a student at the Cranbrook Academy and studied under Eliel Saarinen. He subsequently worked for a time with Eero Saarinen before becoming a partner in the San Francisco office of Skidmore, Owings & Merrill. After his death in Mill Valley, California, he was cremated. His ashes are held by family members.

Augustus BAUER
(1827-1894)

Graceland Cemetery,
Chicago, Illinois

Bauer, a prominent architect in Chicago, was also an early employer of Dankmar Adler and George Washington Maher. While large, his marker is a rather ordinary affair that is similar to many other monuments close by.

Alfred N. BEADLE
(1927-1998)

National Memorial Cemetery of Arizona, Phoenix, Arizona

Having served as a Seabee during World War II, Beadle began practicing architecture in Phoenix, Arizona, where, at the age of thirty-seven he designed the then tallest structure in the city, the Executive Towers. He also received attention for his design of Case Study Apartment No. 1 in Phoenix, which was part of John Entenza's Case Study House Project in *Art and Architecture Magazine*. He went on to design buildings in Chicago, Salt Lake City, and Los Angeles.

His burial site is marked with a simple brass plaque.

Welton David BECKET
(1902-1969)

Evergreen Washelli Memorial Park, Seattle, Washington

Born in Seattle, Becket spent most of his career on the West Coast. By the 1950s his firm, Welton Becket Associates, had become one of the largest in the country. In 1987 it merged with Ellerbe Associates to become Ellerbe Becket, a firm that still exists today. Prominent among his many projects are the A-framed Disney Contemporary Resort at Disney World, Florida, and the cylindrical Capital Records Tower in Hollywood, California.

His remains reside in a family plot identified by a large ornamental urn. Marking his site is an elegantly designed rectangle of granite, topped with a bronze plaque bearing his name and dates.

Pietro BELLUSCHI
(1899-1994)

Portland, Oregon

❋ AIA Gold Medal 1972

Born in Italy, Belluschi was trained as an engineer and began his architectural career in Portland, Oregon. When he accepted the deanship of architecture at the Massachusetts Institute of Technology he transferred his Oregon practice to the San Francisco office of Skidmore, Owings & Merrill. His most famous works are the Equitable Building in Portland, Oregon, and the Cathedral of St. Mary of the Assumption in San Francisco. Belluschi wanted neither a service nor a marker after his death, so his cremated remains are held privately by a family member.

Solon BEMAN
(1853-1914)

Oak Woods Cemetery, Chicago, Illinois

Beman was the designer of the Pullman community in Chicago as well as several First Church of Christ, Scientist, churches throughout the country. Beman's family plot is marked with a stubby obelisk. Nearby is a headstone showing the names of both Beman and his wife that mimics those of other family members who are buried there.

Asher BENJAMIN
(1773-1845)

Mt. Auburn Cemetery,
Cambridge, Massachusetts

Edward BENNETT
(1874-1954)

Lake Forest Cemetery,
Lake Forest, Illinois

Benjamin rose from simple roots, with no formal education, to become a highly regarded expert in Federal style and, later, Greek Revival style architecture. He graduated from simply building structures as a "housewright" to designing them. He is best known for his seven pattern books of architectural details and plans, which had a profound impact on the look of buildings throughout America up to the Civil War.

His marker is an elegant bronze plaque bearing the names and dates of Benjamin and his wife along with three of his children. The plaque is mounted on a rough-hewn granite boulder.

Bennett was a collaborator with Daniel Burnham in the development of the Chicago Plan of 1909. His marker is a ledger that covers his burial vault and is similar to those of other family members. Nearby is the grave of his son, Edward Bennett, Jr., also an architect.

Richard BENNETT
(1891-1974)

Mt. Auburn Cemetery,
Cambridge, Massachusetts

Louise BETHUNE
(1856-1913)

Forest Lawn Cemetery,
Buffalo, New York

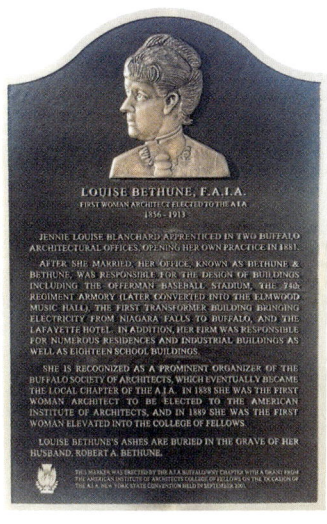

Bennett studied architecture at Harvard and went on to teach at Columbia Harvard, and Yale, where he served as dean. He also was a partner in the Chicago firm of Loebl, Schlossman, Bennett & Dart, where he designed several trend-setting shopping centers.

Unlike most of his peers, Bennett left quite specific instructions regarding what was to be done with his ashes, and his family followed those wishes as best they could. His cremated remains were divided among several sites that were important to him, including the Old Orchard Shopping Center and 1350 North Lake Shore Drive, both in Chicago and both designed by him, and at the site of his summer cottage in Dune Acres, Indiana. The largest portion of his remains was interred beneath a simple stone disk that notes his dates and profession.

After apprenticing with other architects, Bethune and her husband opened an architectural office in 1881. By so doing, she is credited with being the country's first professional woman architect. Despite her importance, she is buried next to her husband beneath a headstone bearing only his name. Acknowledging this oversight, the local chapter of the American Institute of Architects arranged for the installation of a nearby plaque that proclaims her accomplishments and significance.

James BOGARDUS
(1800-1874)

Green-Wood Cemetery,
Brooklyn, New York

Bogardus is best known for his use of cast iron, both as a structural element and as a facade treatment. His grave is marked with an obelisk bearing his name. More recently, a local historic group placed a brass plaque in front of this monument that tells of Borgardus's many accomplishments.

William W. BOYINGTON
(1818-1898)

Rosehill Cemetery,
Chicago, Illinois

Boyington was an influential architect in the Midwest during a time of rapid expansion in the late nineteenth century. One of his designs was the Chicago Water Tower, which survived the Chicago Fire of 1871 and still stands proudly today.

His grave, along with that of his wife, is marked with a simple headstone.

Marcel BREUER
(1902-1981)

Wellfleet, Massachusetts

❦ AIA Gold Medal 1968

Part of the Bauhaus movement in Germany, Breuer immigrated to the United States and maintained an ongoing relationship with Walter Gropius. He established what became a significant architectural practice, designing residences, churches, schools, and office buildings.

Breuer's cremated remains are buried beneath a block of granite on the property of the residence he designed for himself. The markings on the stone are hard to decipher but apparently were chosen by the self-deprecating Breuer to say, "Here lies Breuer who broke his knee entirely of his own stupidity."

Jacques BROWNSON
(1923-2012)

Logan National Cemetery, Denver, Colorado, and Graceland Cemetery, Chicago, Illinois

Brownson studied architecture at the Illinois Institute of Technology under Mies van der Rohe. That influence is easily seen in his masterpiece, the Richard J. Daley Center in Chicago, which he designed while chief of design at C. F. Murphy Associates. In his oral history, Brownson noted that Mies said to him, referring to the Daley Center, "I wish I had done that" and "I couldn't have done better myself." In 1966, he left the firm of CFMA in order to teach and follow other pursuits. He ultimately moved to Colorado, where he died several years later. Brownson's cremated remains are within a military cemetery behind a stone slab noting only his military credentials, neglecting to make any reference to his importance as an architect.

In 2013 a cenotaph was installed at Graceland Cemetery, close to markers of other noted architects of Brownson's time, including Bruce Graham, Fazlur Khan, Stanislaw Gladych, Walter Netsch, and Ludwig Mies van der Rohe.

Leroy BUFFINGTON
(1847-1931)

Lakewood Cemetery,
Minneapolis, Minnesota

Buffington was an early designer of high-rise office towers throughout the Midwest. His grave bears a simple marker identical to that of his wife and lies within a larger family plot.

Charles BULFINCH
(1763-1844)

Mt. Auburn Cemetery,
Cambridge, Massachusetts

Bulfinch practiced architecture in the Boston area in the early nineteenth century, designing such structures as the Massachusetts State House and a later design for the United States Capitol. His gravesite is marked with a stately monument capped with a large stone urn. Unlike the understated markers of many of his fellow architects, Bulfinch's numerous accomplishments are boldly delineated on his monument.

Gordon BUNSHAFT
(1909-1990)

Temple Beth El Cemetery, Buffalo, New York

Bunshaft was the senior design partner in the New York office of Skidmore, Owings & Merrill during the booming 1950s and 1960s. He is credited with opening the modern age of skyscrapers with his design for the iconic Lever House on Park Avenue in New York in 1952. This building was hailed by architectural historian Lewis Mumford, who described the building as having "all that can be said, delicately, accurately, elegantly, with surfaces of glass, with ribs of steel … an impeccable achievement." The Beinecke Library at Yale University was another of his stellar achievements.

He was born in Buffalo, New York, and attended the Massachusetts Institute of Technology. After working briefly with Edward Durell Stone, he joined Skidmore, Owings & Merrill, remaining there for the rest of his career. He received many awards, including the Gold Medal from the American Academy and Institute of Arts and Letters (1984) and the Pritzker Architecture Prize (1984).

His remains are buried in a large family plot in his hometown. Before his death, he collaborated with the monument maker on the design of his headstone and those of nearby family members.

Daniel Hudson BURNHAM
(1846-1912)

Graceland Cemetery, Chicago, Illinois

there was a natural connection with the cemetery. His marker, a rough-hewn boulder with a simple brass plaque, likely was created collaboratively between Simonds and the Burnham family. Besides Burnham himself, his wife and four children are buried on the island with markers similar to Burnham's. Two of his sons, Daniel, Jr., and Hubert, were also architects who carried on the Burnham name for several years.

Burnham's firm was well known for its design of many buildings throughout the country. Burnham was also renowned as a city planner, designing master plans for cities such as Chicago, San Francisco, Cleveland, and Manila, the Philippines, as well as the plan for the mall in Washington, D.C.

His cremated remains are located on a bucolic island in the middle of Lake Willowmere, within Graceland Cemetery. It is significant that in a cemetery filled with Chicago's richest and most famous, including Marshall Field, Potter Palmer, and George Pullman, one of the most prominent sites has been given to a mere architect. Perhaps none of the prominent families at Graceland was interested in the site because it was relatively small and bodies had to be cremated because of the high water table. The original plan of Ossian Simonds, the superintendent and planner for the cemetery for many years, was to leave the island natural and undeveloped. Upon Burnham's sudden and unexpected death at the height of his fame in 1912, it is likely that the cemetery offered this site to the Burnham family. Burnham's parents are interred at Graceland, so

Barry BYRNE
(1883-1967)

Calvary Cemetery,
Evanston, Illinois

Though he dropped out of grade school, Byrne became a proficient architect while working for Frank Lloyd Wright in Oak Park, Illinois. He later worked for Walter Burley Griffin and is credited with finishing several of Griffin's

projects after Griffin moved to Australia to work on his Canberra capital-city plans. Byrne went on to design buildings for several Catholic parishes throughout the country. His and his wife's spaces in the cemetery were given to him in trade for his designing the cemetery's office building. His burial site bears a simple headstone with his name and dates.

Alfred CALDWELL
(1903-1998)

Bristol, Wisconsin

Recognized for his landscape designs and his close association with Mies van der Rohe, Caldwell was a colorful personality known for the white suits he often wore and was a popular teacher at the Illinois Institute of Technology. The landscaping design for the Mies's housing project, Lafayette Park, in Detroit is one of his most highly regarded projects.

His cremated remains are scattered at his personal residence in rural Wisconsin with no marker.

Eduardo CATALANO
(1917-2010)

Buenos Aires, Argentina

Catalano is another example of a non-American architect who had significant impact on this country's architectural development. Raised in Argentina, Catalano studied architecture in Buenos Aires, in London, and in the United States at the University of Pennsylvania and Harvard University. After Matthew Nowicki's untimely death, Catalano became professor of architecture at North Carolina State University, Raleigh, North Carolina, where he designed his own home, which included a wooden hyperbolic-paraboloid roof and glass walls. It received national attention and became his best-known work, receiving praise even from Frank Lloyd Wright.

Catalano then moved on to the Massachusetts Institute of Technology where he headed the graduate program in architecture for many years. He went on to design the Juilliard School of Music in New York, as well as U.S. embassies in Buenos Aires and Pretoria, South Africa.

After his death in Cambridge, Massachusetts, most of his ashes were interred in the family mausoleum he designed in La Chacarita Cemetery in Buenos Aires. The rest were deposited at the large public sculpture, Floralis Generica, which he designed for the plaza of the United Nations in his native city. The petals of this metal sculpture open each morning and close each evening.

Serge CHERMAYEFF
(1900-1996)

Wellfleet, Massachusetts

Chermayeff, an architect and designer, was born in Russia. He was educated and practiced in England before immigrating to the United States in 1940. On the recommendation of Walter Gropius, he became director of the Institute of Design, which ultimately merged into the Illinois Institute of Technology. He went on to teach at Yale, MIT, and Harvard Universities and had a significant impact on students matriculating through those institutions.

His ashes were deposited in the Atlantic Ocean at Wellfleet, Massachusetts, where he had lived.

Henry S. CHURCHILL
(1893-1962)

Philadelphia, Pennsylvania

Churchill was trained as an architect at Cornell University but is known primarily for his work as a city planner. His book *The City Is the People* is considered a classic. He was the planner for several communities in the Philadelphia area and across the country and was influential in guiding important national housing legislation.

A family member believes that his ashes were deposited on the grounds of his house in the Philadelphia area.

Henry Ives COBB
(1859-1931)

Green-Wood Cemetery, Brooklyn, New York

Born in Massachusetts, Cobb spent most of his professional life in Chicago, teaming up with partner Charles Frost. Cobb's grave is marked with a simple headstone, similar to that of his wife, who lies alongside.

Charles Allerton COOLIDGE
(1858-1936)

Mt. Auburn Cemetery, Cambridge, Massachusetts

Coolidge was a partner in the firm Shepley, Rutan & Coolidge, which succeeded the firm of H. H. Richardson after Richardson's death. The firm went on to design major projects throughout the country. Coolidge and his wife, the sister of his partner George Shepley, are buried within a plot marked by a large stone tablet. Coolidge's actual grave bears a simple marker showing only his initials and date of death.

Ralph Adams CRAM
(1863-1944)

St. Elizabeth's Church Chapel, Sudbury, Massachusetts

Cram is known for the many churches and university campuses that he designed. Among his credits are the campuses of the United States Military Academy at West Point, New York, Princeton University, and Rice University.

His gravesite is one of the loveliest of all that were visited. A walk along a path through tall pine trees leads one to a small, rustic chapel designed by Cram. Cram had purchased several acres of this land, along with an old farmhouse, which he and his family used as a summer retreat. He ultimately built this simple stone chapel with the help of family members and local stonemasons. He described it as "perhaps the most satisfactory church I have ever built." The chapel and land were deeded to a local church with the condition that his grave could be placed next to the chapel. Thus, adjacent to this rustic chapel are two blue slate headstones and footstones facing the chapel's entrance that note the graves of Cram and his wife.

It is noteworthy that Cram is one of the few architects who put such care and thought into the marker and site where his remains would be placed.

Paul CRET
(1876-1945)

Woodlands Cemetery, Philadelphia, Pennsylvania

❁ AIA Gold Medal 1938

Edward DART
(1922-1975)

St. Michael's Episcopal Church, Barrington, Illinois

Born in Lyon, France, Cret was trained at that city's Ecole des Beaux-Arts and went on to further study in Paris. He came to the United States in 1903 to teach at the University of Pennsylvania. At the outbreak of World War I, he enlisted with the French army and was made an officer in the Legion of Honor. After the war he returned to the United States for the rest of his career; he designed several significant projects including the Folger Shakespeare Library in Washington, D.C., the Cincinnati Union Terminal in that city, and the master plan for the University of Texas in Austin.

His architectural style, though based on the Beaux-Arts tradition, simplified classical motifs into something almost abstract. He taught for thirty years at the University of Pennsylvania, where one of his students and employees was Louis Kahn.

To reach Cret's gravesite, one passes through majestic cemetery gates that were designed by Cret. His grave is marked by a simple bronze plaque.

Dart grew up in New Orleans and attended the University of Virginia before joining the U.S. Navy at the outbreak of World War II. He became a pilot who saw action in the Pacific during the war. After his return, he enrolled in the Yale University architecture program, where he studied under such luminaries as Eero Saarinen and Pietro Belluschi. Upon graduation he worked for Skidmore, Owings & Merrill and Edward Durell Stone for a short time before opening his own architectural office. It was there that he designed over 200 projects. Despite having a robust architectural practice, he strived for larger projects than the residences and churches in which his firm specialized. He therefore joined the firm of Loebl, Schlossman & Bennett in Chicago, where he designed the Pick-Staiger Concert Hall in Evanston, Illinois, and Chicago's Water Tower Place, one of the first mixed use projects in the country, combining retail, a hotel, and residences in one structure.

His cremated remains were installed behind a brass plaque at St. Michaels Episcopal Church which he designed in Barrington, Illinois.

Julius Ralph (J. R.) DAVIDSON
(1889-1973)

Ojia, California

Along with designers such as Neutra, Elwood, Koenig, and Lautner, Davidson is credited with having created in southern California after World War II the prototype for modern, casual, and visually exciting low-cost housing. Born in Berlin, Germany, Davidson studied and worked there until moving to Los Angeles, California, in 1923. His first activity in the United States was designing sets for motion-picture director Cecil B. DeMille. From there he went on to design several houses during the 1930s and 1940s. He was invited to participate in John Entenza's Case Study House Project, designing the highly regarded House No. 1. Despite his many projects, Davidson was never licensed as an architect.

Davidson spent his final years in his home in Ojia, California. It is there that his ashes were spread beneath a tree that he treasured.

Natalie DE BLOIS
(1921-2013)

Lake Michigan

After receiving her degree in architecture from Columbia University, de Blois spent many years at Skidmore, Owings & Merrill in New York and Chicago. While there she had important design roles in several of the firm's major buildings, such as Lever House, the Pepsi Cola Building, and the Union Carbide Building, along with the Connecticut General Building for its New York office and the Equitable Building for its Chicago office. She received little acknowledgment for her role in these projects except from Nathaniel Owings, who gave her great praise in his autobiography, *The Spaces in Between*.

She died in Chicago and her ashes were deposited in Lake Michigan near Promontory Point, where she loved to swim.

William Adams DELANO
(1874-1960)

St. John's Memorial Cemetery, Nassau County, New York

 AIA Gold Medal 1953

Born of socially prominent parents, Delano was educated at Yale University and at the Ecole des Beaux-Arts in Paris. He was a long-time partner of Chester Holmes Aldrich in the firm of Delano & Aldrich. Having connections with many of the East Coast's wealthy families, the firm designed a series of buildings for the Rockefellers, Astors, Vanderbilts, and Whitneys.

Delano's gravesite bears a stone marker with a bronze plaque calling out his name and dates.

Frederick DINKELBERG
(1858-1934)

Wunder's Cemetery, Chicago, Illinois

Dinkelberg was a designer for the firm of D. H. Burnham & Company and is credited with assisting Daniel Burnham with plans for the 1893 Columbian Exposition as well as the designs for the Gas Building in Chicago and the Flatiron Building in New York City. During the Great Depression, Dinkelberg lost virtually all of the wealth he had amassed; he and his wife were on public welfare at the time of his death. The local chapter of the American Institute of Architects provided funds for his burial and for his headstone in a somewhat forlorn cemetery just across the street from Graceland Cemetery, where a multitude of his peers reside.

Ford Foundation Building in New York City. His burial site is marked with a simple tablet bearing his and his wife's names and dates.

John Gerard DINKELOO
(1918-1981)

Central Burying Grounds,
Hamden, Connecticut

Alden DOW
(1904-1983)

Midland Cemetery,
Midland, Michigan

Dinkeloo worked in Eero Saarinen's office until Saarinen's death. He and Kevin Roche, another employee of Saarinen's, went on to form the firm Roche Dinkeloo, which designed many important buildings, including the

A member of the prominent Dow family, founders of Dow Chemical, Alden Dow turned to architecture as a young man, practicing for a while in his hometown of Midland, Michigan, before studying under Frank Lloyd Wright at Taliesin in Spring Green, Wisconsin. He returned to Midland and, assisted by his family connections, was able to undertake several significant commissions throughout Michigan.

His grave is located within the family plot at Midland Cemetery. His marker seems to overwhelm the graves of his powerful forebears. Here is a case where a mere architect upstages some of the most powerful industrialists in the country. The monument itself was designed after Dow's death by Bill Gilmore, a partner in the firm of Dow-Howell-Gilmore.

William DRUMMOND
(1876-1946)

Forest Home Cemetery,
Forest Park, Illinois

When he was ten, Drummond and his family moved from Newark, New Jersey, to Chicago. After attending Chicago public schools he completed only a year at the University of Illinois because of financial constraints. He took a drafting job in Louis Sullivan's firm before moving on to become chief draftsman in Frank Lloyd Wright's office. He was there during the time (1905-1909) that Wright produced many of his most important Prairie Style projects.

After leaving Wright in 1909, Drummond opened his own office and designed several Prairie Style residences in the Chicago area. When popularity of the Prairie Style faded in the 1920s, Drummond's designs moved toward more traditional historic styles. His practice was severely affected by the Great Depression, and he never recovered his former prominence as an architect. Many of his later projects are in River Forest, Illinois, where he resided.

Drummond is buried beneath a simple bronze plaque.

James EADS
(1820-1887)

Bellefontaine Cemetery,
St. Louis, Missouri

As an engineer, Eads was responsible for many important works, including the remarkable 6,400-foot span bridge in St. Louis (1874) that bears his name. His marker is an ornate sarcophagus.

Charles EAMES
(1909-1978)
and Ray EAMES
(1912-1988)

Calvary Cemetery,
St. Louis, Missouri

Charles and Ray Eames were a husband and wife team who met at the Cranbrook Academy of Art in Bloomfield Hills, Michigan. While there the Eameses were exposed to the influence of the school's founder, Finnish architect Eliel Saarinen, and can be seen in many of their designs. They also became life-long friends with Eliel Saarinen's son, Eero. Later, Eero Saarinen said that Charles Eames, along with his father and Matthew Nowicki, were the biggest influences in his life.

The Eameses worked together for virtually their entire careers, designing buildings as well as many well-known pieces of furniture. Their cremated remains bear no markers and reside quietly and anonymously within the Eames family plot.

Harvey ELLIS
(1852-1904)

St. Agnes Cemetery,
Syracuse, New York

Ellis was an enigmatic architect and artist who worked for such luminaries as H. H. Richardson, Leroy Buffington, Gustav Stickley, and possibly Louis Sullivan. Many believe that some of the works of these giants were actually the creations of Ellis. However, his abuse of alcohol and elusive personality prevented him from ever receiving proper credit for his many sizeable contributions.

Much as he was overlooked in life, his gravesite was neglected for many years until a group of his admirers arranged to have the current marker installed.

Craig ELLWOOD
(1922-1992)

Pergine Valdarno, Italy

Ellwood was an influential Los Angeles based mid-century modernist whose designs combined the informality of Californian modernism with the more rigid International style as expressed by Mies van der Rohe in his designs.

Ellwood, born Jon Nelson Burke, moved with his family when he was a teen from Texas to the Los Angeles area. After serving in WWII as a bomber radio operator, he returned to California to set up a construction business. It was there that he legally changed his name to Craig Ellwood, the name supposedly coming from a liquor store with a similar name near his fledgling business.

In 1951 he established Craig Ellwood Design and went on to win several major commissions, both residential and commercial, including the Rand Corporation Headquarters in Santa Monica, California, and office buildings for IBM and Xerox. His firm also designed three houses for the Case Study House Project. Interestingly, despite Ellwood's fame as a designer and lecturer, he never was licensed as an architect but always had a staff of registered architects working for him.

Ellwood retired to Italy to paint and it was there that he died. His cremated remains, along with those of what apparently was a highly regarded pet dog, reside in a wall at a small country cemetery in Tuscany, Italy.

George Grant ELMSLIE
(1871-1952)

Graceland Cemetery,
Chicago, Illinois

A prolific architect, mainly of residences, Elmslie worked for many years with partner architect William Purcell. Both Purcell and Elmslie had been employed by Louis Sullivan. Many of their buildings are in the Prairie Style, reflecting the profound influence of Frank Lloyd Wright. When the Prairie Style fell out of favor in the 1920s, Elmslie's designs evolved into more traditional styles.

Elmslie is buried within the family plot of his wife's family, the Hunters. A large granite tablet memorializes the names of his wife's parents, his wife, his brother-in-law, and Elmslie.

Joseph ESHERICK
(1914-1998)

Sausalito, California

 AIA Gold Medal 1989

Joseph Esherick graduated from the University of Pennsylvania after learning much about wood craftsmanship from his uncle, sculptor Wharton Esherick. He set up practice in the San Francisco area in 1953 and taught at the University of California, Berkeley, for many years. While there, he, with William Wurster and Vernon DeMars, founded the influential College of Environmental Design.

He designed many houses and university buildings in the bay area that reflect the traditions of Bernard Maybeck. He is probably best known for the Cannery Project in San Francisco.

His ashes were scattered on the oceanfront at Fort Cronkite near Sausalito, California.

Ulrich FRANZEN
(1921-2012)

Santa Fe, New Mexico

Franzen was born in Germany, immigrated to the United States, and attended graduate school at Harvard. After working for a short time for I. M. Pei, he went on to form his own firm, which designed several significant buildings around the country.

There is no marker for Franzen. His ashes were scattered around the house that he designed for himself in Santa Fe.

Albert FREY
(1903-1998)

Welwood Murray Cemetery, Palm Springs, California

Born in Zurich, Switzerland, Frey received his architecture diploma from the Institute of Technology in Winterthur. He spent two years as assistant to Le Corbusier, during which time he worked on the iconic Villa Savoye.

Frey came to the United States in 1928, as the first architect to have worked for Le Corbusier.

In collaboration with Lawrence Kocker, editor of *Architectural Record*, he designed the Aluminaire House in 1931. It showed the influence of Le Corbusier and was included in the seminal 1932 MoMA International Style Exhibition. This building was later purchased by Wallace Harrison and has since been dismantled with the intention of relocating it to Palm Springs, California, as a memorial to Frey; it is where much of his later, mostly residential, work is located and where he is buried.

His marker is a simple plaque noting his dates and his having been an architect.

Charles FROST
(1856-1931)

Rosehill Cemetery,
Chicago, Illinois

Frost and his partner, Alfred Granger, designed many buildings for the Chicago & Northwestern Railroad. Both Frost and Granger were sons-in-law of Marvin Hughitt, the president of the railroad, thus explaining why Frost and Granger had so many railroad commissions.

The importance of Hughitt to Frost's and Granger's careers is memorialized by the fact that both architects are buried in their father-in-law's family plot, which is marked with a large obelisk bearing the name Hughitt. Within this plot, Frost's grave, alongside Granger's, is marked with a simple headstone.

Henry Atherton FROST
(1883-1952)

Mt. Auburn Cemetery,
Cambridge, Massachusetts

Frost was a long-time and much-admired professor at the Harvard Graduate School of Design. While there, he taught beginning students such as Philip Johnson, John Johansen, and Edward Barnes. His grave is marked with a large stone monument bearing the family name.

Buckminster FULLER
(1895-1983)

Mt. Auburn Cemetery,
Cambridge, Massachusetts

✣ AIA Gold Medal 1970

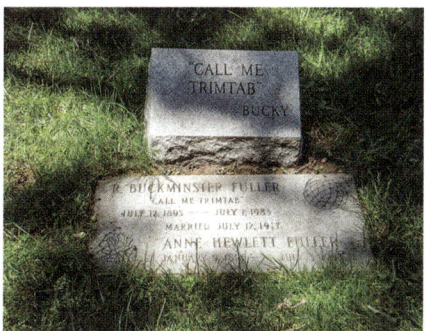

Fuller is known for his development of the geodesic dome and other futuristic concepts that involved everything from prefab housing to automobiles. The United States Postal Service issued a postage stamp in his honor in 2004.

He is buried in his family's plot with a marker incorporating a geodesic dome and his epitaph, "Call me Trimtab"—a term Fuller often used as a metaphor for leadership and personal empowerment. In sailing and aviation, trim tabs are devices attached to major control surfaces that, despite their small size, can have a significant impact on the overall heading of the craft being controlled.

Frank FURNESS
(1839-1912)

Laurel Hill Cemetery,
Philadelphia, Pennsylvania

Furness was an extraordinarily colorful personality who was not only a highly influential architectural designer but also a distinguished officer in the American Civil War. Much of his important work in the late nineteenth century centered on the Philadelphia area. Young architects who worked for him, such as Louis Sullivan, were highly influenced by his unique design concepts.

During the Civil War, Furness reached the rank of captain and was awarded the Congressional Medal of Honor for his valor. Curiously, his grave, located within a family plot, is marked only with a military headstone noting his having received the Congressional Medal of Honor but forgoing any mention of his significant architectural accomplishments.

Cass GILBERT
(1859-1934)

Fairlawn Cemetery, Ridgefield, Connecticut

Gilbert had a prolific career, with buildings he designed spanning the country—from the Minnesota State Capitol to the Woolworth Building in New York City.

His gravesite lies within a peaceful hillside cemetery in the middle of a small New England town. Its serene setting on a grassy knoll overlooking the surrounding landscape seems a fitting site for an architect who clearly left a significant mark on the world.

Irving GILL
(1870-1936)

Gill was a key player in the development of the modernist movement in California and was known for the many residences he designed. With no formal education in architecture, he began his career working for Joseph Silsbee, who was also an early employer of Frank Lloyd Wright, and then with Adler and Sullivan in Chicago, where he worked side by side with Wright. He eventually moved to California, where he spent the rest of his career. After his death, he was cremated and his ashes were scattered, so there is no marker for him.

Stanislaw GLADYCH
(1921-1982)

Cmentarz Ewangelicko-Reformowany, Warsaw, Poland

Graceland Cemetery, Chicago, Illinois

Born in Poland, Gladych was captured by the Russians as a teenager during World War II and imprisoned in Siberia. He was released to fight with the Polish forces and became a fighter pilot, being shot down twice. After the war's end, he studied architecture at the Polish School in Liverpool, England before immigrating to the United States and joining the firm of Skidmore, Owings & Merrill in Chicago. While there, he is credited with conceiving the folded-plate motif of the Air Force Academy chapel in Colorado Springs, Colorado. Later on, at the firm of C. F. Murphy Associates, he was responsible for the designs in the Chicago area of O'Hare Airport, the Jardine Filtration Plant, and the First National Bank Building. He also designed the FBI Headquarters Building in Washington, D.C.

Gladych died in Chicago, but his cremated remains are buried in Warsaw, Poland. A marker in his honor was installed in Graceland Cemetery. His site lies among the markers for many of his illustrious peers, including Ludwig Mies van der Rohe, Bruce Graham, Jacques Brownson, and Walter Netsch.

Bruce GOFF
(1904-1982)

Graceland Cemetery,
Chicago, Illinois

Goff is best known for the many houses that he designed, which often defy easy description. His projects have a whimsical quality, frequently involving sharp geometry, dramatic cantilevered roofs, and extensive use of natural materials. Goff was intrigued by Frank Lloyd Wright and corresponded with him for a short time before striking out on his own, ending up at the University of Oklahoma, where he became dean of the school of architecture. Highly charismatic, he developed a devoted following of students and others throughout his life. Besides architecture, Goff dabbled in composing music in which the design of the notes and how they appeared on the page were as important as the sounds created.

Upon Goff's death, his cremated remains were kept by a patron in Oklahoma, Joe Price. Years later, in 2000, an effort was mounted to have Goff's ashes relocated and permanently entombed at Graceland Cemetery in Chicago. Goff's marker was designed by one of his former students, Grant Gustafson, and embodies a unique font that Goff used, as well as a large chunk of glass that is symbolic of the exotic materials Goff often employed in his designs. In this case, the chunk of glass was part of a house he had designed that was destroyed in a fire. An epitaph that Goff imagined for himself ("I had more influence than an alley cat") is not part of his monument.

Myron GOLDSMITH
(1918-1996)

Memorial Park,
Skokie, Illinois

Bertrand GOLDBERG
(1913-1997)

Goldberg was an early student of Mies van der Rohe and many of his early works suggest the influence of his mentor. His later work became more organic, incorporating forms found in nature. His Marina City Towers, based on this concept, have become icons of the Chicago skyline. Ironically, these Goldberg signature buildings are directly adjacent to one of Mies's last and largest buildings, the IBM Tower, showing two distinctly different approaches to high-rise design by two architects who had been closely affiliated earlier in their careers.

Goldberg's cremated remains are in the possession of his family and no final resting place has yet been determined.

Like Bertram Goldberg, Goldsmith was influenced by Mies van der Rohe. In this case, Goldsmith studied under Mies at the Illinois Institute of Technology and worked in Mies's office. He then joined the Chicago office of Skidmore, Owings & Merrill and designed several important buildings while there. He continued teaching at the Illinois Institute of Technology and became interested in bridge design, culminating in his concept for the Ruck-a-Chucky Bridge in California.

Goldsmith left no instructions or design for a permanent marker. A plot in a local cemetery shaded by a large maple tree appealed to the family. The honed absolute-black granite marker was designed by his daughter, Chandra Goldsmith Gray, also an architect. Aware that the material is the same as that used for Mies's marker, she also chose the material because of the gray flannel color that it reflects when honed, a feature that reminds her of her father.

The cited biblical reference speaks of light, which refers to Goldsmith's Hebrew name, Meyer, meaning "light" or "he who illuminates."

Bertram GOODHUE
(1869-1924)

Church of the Intercession, New York, New York

 AIA Gold Medal 1925

Goodhue is best known for his many churches, such as St. Bartholomew's Church in New York City and Rockefeller Chapel in Chicago, and other public buildings, such as the Nebraska State Capitol and the U.S. Military Academy at West Point. His final resting place is one of the grandest of all his peers. His remains are located in a catafalque embedded within a church he designed. Were this church in England, one would expect to see a bishop or a former king in such a place of distinction. In this case, Goodhue is memorialized with a likeness of himself lying on the top of his tomb from where he can survey an overhead arch displaying replicas of his most important buildings. The design for the catafalque was done by Lee Lawrie, an associate of Goodhue on many projects. It is unknown whether Goodhue planned to be entombed at this church or whether he had any input into his grave's design. Nevertheless, what resulted is certainly one of the grandest tributes that can be bestowed upon any architect—a truly regal monument within a building that he had designed.

Bruce GRAHAM
(1925-2010)

Tequesta, Florida

Graceland Cemetery, Chicago, Illinois

Graham was the senior design partner at Skidmore, Owings & Merrill in Chicago for many years and was involved with several of the important buildings that flowed from that office during his tenure, including Chicago's Sears Tower and John Hancock Building.

Graham died in Florida, where his remains are interred with those of his wife. That site was designed by Graham and his wife prior to her death. The rather conventional exedra was added after her death by Graham. However, his family wanted a marker in Chicago as well, owing to his close association with the city and his long-time professional collaboration with fellow SOM partner Fazlur Khan. Thus, Graham's cenotaph, designed by Craig Hartman in the SOM office, lies directly next to Khan's marker, which, in fact, Graham himself had designed earlier. The Graham marker is in close harmony with the earlier Khan marker in terms of size, materials, and placement. His marker incorporates a black concave "vessel" that floats atop an anchored green earth stone. The intent is for his name to "float" above the surface of the water that would collect naturally. In the cold light of reality this concept has not worked out as planned, since the vessel collects leaves and other debris as readily as the intended rainwater.

Ernest GRAHAM
(1868-1936)

Graceland Cemetery, Chicago, Illinois

Graham was a partner in the prolific firm of Graham, Anderson, Probst & White, which designed major buildings throughout the country. Graham was born in Michigan and failed to graduate from high school, from which he had been expelled as a result of bad conduct. His father put him to work as an apprentice bricklayer and he plied that trade until eventually finding work with a local architectural office. In 1888, he moved to Chicago, a wildly growing metropolis at the time, and found work as a construction superintendent for architects Holabird & Roche. He was recommended by William Holabird to Daniel Burnham who had just been appointed chief of construction for the Columbian World Exposition. At the age of twenty-four, he had so impressed Burnham that he was made assistant chief of construction at the exposition.

At the exposition's conclusion, Graham joined the Burnham firm and, in 1904, was made a partner. When Burnham died unexpectedly in 1912, Graham reorganized the firm into what eventually became Graham, Anderson, Probst & White, a firm renowned for major buildings across the country that include the Merchandise Mart and the Wrigley Building, in Chicago, the Equitable Building in New York, and Union Station in Washington, D.C.

After his death, Graham's estate was used to establish the Graham Foundation for Advanced Studies in the Fine Arts, which remains today as the foremost private provider of funding for architecture-related study projects. Graham's marker is a simple headstone next to that of his wife.

Alfred GRANGER
(1867-1939)

Rosehill Cemetery,
Chicago, Illinois

Granger was a partner with Charles Frost in the firm Frost & Granger. Both married daughters of the railroad magnate Marvin Hughitt, president of the Chicago & Northwestern Railroad. The firm went on to design many stations for that railroad. Both Frost and Granger are buried, along with their wives, in the family plot of their father-in-law, Marvin Hughitt.

Michael GRAVES
(1934-2015)

Princeton Cemetery,
Princeton, New Jersey

 AIA Gold Medal 2001

Graves was born and grew up in Cincinnati, Ohio. After undergraduate work at the University of Cincinnati, he went on to receive his master's degree in architecture from Harvard University.

He established his firm, Michael Graves & Associates, in Princeton, New Jersey. Early in his career he espoused an architectural style that expressed modernism in its purist form. However, his interest changed and he became one of the leaders of the postmodernist movement. The Portland Building, Portland, Oregon, the Denver Public Library, and the Humana Building, Louisville, Kentucky, dramatically demonstrated his new design direction.

Besides architecture, Graves established himself as a gifted designer of household products. In an alliance with the Italian design firm Alessi, Graves designed a line of products that were sold in retail stores such as Target and J. C. Penney.

In 2003, Graves became partially paralyzed as the result of a spinal infection. Though confined to a wheelchair he remained active and a vital part of the design world until his death.

His grave marker was created by one of his associates, Donald Strum, and is based on sketches that Graves had done for an exhibit that the office was preparing at the time of his death. The marker of red granite incorporates several reference to the postmodern style with which Graves was so closely identified.

Charles Sumner GREENE
(1868-1957)

Monterey Cemetery,
Monterey, California

Charles Greene and his brother, Henry Greene, spent virtually their entire lives together. Born in Ohio, they studied at the Massachusetts Institute of Technology and worked at a series of architectural firms in the East until, at the urging of their parents to join them, they moved to California. It was there that they ultimately established the firm of Greene & Greene, which created an extraordinary array of Arts and Crafts style houses.

Greene and his wife are buried beneath a stone marker bearing their dates.

same schools and worked for the same firms until setting up their own practice at Greene & Greene. It was there that they designed the Arts and Crafts masterpieces for which they are famous.

The graves of Henry Greene and his wife are marked with simple headstones that reportedly were designed by Greene himself.

Henry Mather GREENE
(1870-1954)

San Gabriel Cemetery,
San Gabriel, California

The life of Henry Greene was profoundly intertwined with that of his brother, Charles. Both attended the

Walter Burley GRIFFIN
(1876-1937)

Nishatganj Cemetery,
Lucknow, India

Griffin had a long and prolific career. In his early years he was an associate of Frank Lloyd Wright, and his design influence can be seen in some of Wright's residential work during that period. After leaving Wright's office in 1906, he designed several residences as well as three residential communities in the Chicago area and Iowa. He and his wife, Marion Mahony (Griffin), won the Canberra capital-city design competition in 1912 and moved to Australia to supervise the project. Some say that had he stayed in Chicago his fame and prominence might have rivaled that of Frank Lloyd Wright. Their time in Australia was highly stressful and ultimately they left for India, where they set to work on several projects.

It is there that Griffin died and was buried. His monument, installed years after his death, consists of a stone ledger with a large headstone bearing a plaque inscribed with his name and dates. The site is bordered by an iron fence.

Walter GROPIUS
(1883-1969)

Stansdorf, Germany

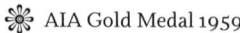 AIA Gold Medal 1959

Gropius founded the famous Bauhaus school of design in Germany in 1919 and headed it until 1928. He moved to the United States in 1937 to teach at the Harvard Graduate School of Design and became chair of its Department of Architecture, where he remained for many years. During that time he designed several buildings throughout the country, many in collaboration with Marcel Breuer, with whom he had worked at the Bauhaus.

Gropius's ashes were returned to Germany upon his death and were scattered at a Jewish cemetery in Stansdorf, Germany.

Victor GRUEN
(1903-1980)

Vienna, Austria

Gruen (né Grünbaum) was born in Vienna, Austria, and received his architectural training there. As a young man he showed strong talents for singing and acting. He also became an outspoken Socialist. Reportedly he directed a small cabaret theater where satires about Hitler and his expansionist goals were produced. In these productions Gruen apparently donned a Nazi uniform and aped Hitler's speeches. When alerted that the Gestapo was looking for him in 1938, he put on a Nazi lieutenant's uniform and escaped to an airfield, where he successfully fled to the United States.

In New York City he built his architectural practice by designing shops and display spaces. In 1941 he moved to Los Angeles, where he began the firm, Victor Gruen Associates. For better or worse, that firm is credited with having pioneered the modern suburban shopping mall. The first of these was the Southdale Mall in Minneapolis in 1956. Malcolm Gladwell reportedly said, because of the proliferation of suburban malls, that Gruen may be the most influential architect of the twentieth century.

Gruen returned to Vienna in 1968 where he remarried and where he remained until his death. His children believe that his ashes were placed at one of the locations he loved in Vienna.

Charles GWATHMEY
(1938-2009)

Green River Cemetery,
East Hampton, New York

Zaha HADID
(1950-2016)

Brookwood Cemetery,
Woking, Surrey, England

Gwathmey and his architectural partner, Robert Siegel, headed a firm that designed significant buildings throughout the country. He is buried in a small cemetery on eastern Long Island that is noted for being the final resting place of many significant artists, including Jackson Pollock and Willem de Kooning.

Hadid was an Iraqi-born British architect who gained early recognition for her distinctively futuristic designs characterized by curling forms and broken geometry. She studied under Rem Koolhaas in London and later worked for him in Amsterdam. Her designs in the United States include the Broad Art Museum at Michigan State University and the Rosenthal Center for Contemporary Art in Cincinnati. She was the first woman to be awarded the renowned Pritzker Prize.

Hadid died abruptly of a heart attack in Miami, Florida, and was buried beside her father and brother in the Muslim section of the Brookwood Cemetery in England. A permanent marker for her will be erected on this site in the future.

Stratton HAMMON
(1904-1997)

Cave Hill Cemetery,
Louisville, Kentucky

Hammon was an architect with no formal architectural training. Nevertheless, he went on to design scores of residences, many quite large and prestigious, primarily in the Louisville area, which embody sophisticated colonial and Georgian design motifs. His site is marked with a ledger that goes into extensive and glowing detail about his life and family. Perhaps this was to make up for what he may have seen as weakness in his academic credentials.

Harwell Hamilton HARRIS
(1903-1990)

Carmel, California

A modernist architect, Harris combined Arts and Crafts elements into his many residential works. Since Harris gave no instructions prior to his death about what was to be done with his cremated remains, it was decided to scatter his ashes in the Carmel River where it joins the Pacific Ocean. This is the site of one of his important works, the Marian Lawrence Clark House.

Wallace HARRISON
(1895-1981)

Sleepy Hollow Cemetery,
Sleepy Hollow, New York

 AIA Gold Medal 1967

Hartman was a partner in the Chicago office of Skidmore, Owings & Merrill. Among his many achievements he is credited with bringing the great unnamed sculpture by Pablo Picasso to the Daley Center Plaza in Chicago. A simple stone marker notes Hartman's gravesite.

Harrison was a partner in the New York firm of Harrison & Abramowitz, which designed large projects throughout the country, including office towers, museums, and auditoriums. Rockefeller Center, the United Nations Secretariat Building, and the Governor Nelson A. Rockefeller Empire State Plaza are some of his major projects. The location of Harrison's ashes is noted with a marker installed by his family several years after his death.

Sophia HAYDEN (BENNETT)
(1868-1953)

Massachusetts

Hayden was born in Santiago, Chile. Her American father sent her to live with her grandparents in Boston at the age of six so that she could be schooled there. She soon developed a strong interest in architecture. Hayden became the first woman to receive a degree in architecture from the Massachusetts Institute of Technology. When she was twenty-one, her entry won the competition to design the Woman's Building at the Columbian Exposition in Chicago in 1893. Regrettably, this is the only significant structure she ever designed, and she soon moved away from practicing architecture, presumably because of the difficulty she had making any headway as a woman in what was then a man's profession.

Hayden died in Winthrop, Massachusetts, and was cremated. There is no record of any marker for her.

William HARTMANN
(1916-2003)

Castine Town Cemetery, Castine, Maine

John Q. HEJDUK
(1929-2000)

Oakland Cemetery,
Yonkers, New York

Hejduk was a visionary architect and educator. He was dean of the architecture school at Cooper Union in New York for several years, where he assembled a faculty that produced a number of students who subsequently had prominent careers.

His drawings and his many theoretical constructions are legendary, but he also was a practical architect as demonstrated by his reconstruction of the Cooper Union Foundation Building and such projects as the Kreutzberg Tower in Berlin and the Wall House II in Groningen, the Netherlands.

The design of Hejduk's gravestone was adapted from one of his last drawings. The two crosses were not intended for a gravestone, yet they are appropriate, even providential, in that Hejduk's son, Rafael, died only a few weeks after his father and is buried with him.

James HOBAN
(1762-1831)

Mt. Olivet Cemetery,
Washington, D.C

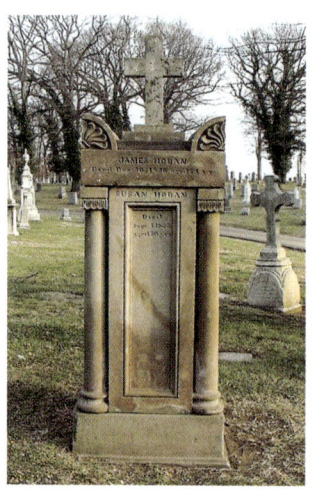

An immigrant from Ireland, Hoban is most noted for being the architect of the White House in Washington, D.C. Hoban was honored by postage stamps of the same design issued in 1981 by both the United States and Ireland.

His grave is marked with a monument that embodies several classical elements.

John Augur HOLABIRD
(1886-1945)

Graceland Cemetery,
Chicago, Illinois

The plot is marked with a block of red granite bearing the family name. Laid out before this marker are the individual headstones of the family members, all of the same simple design.

John Augur HOLABIRD, JR.
(1920-2009)

Graceland Cemetery,
Chicago, Illinois

As the son of the founder of an architectural family dynasty, Holabird formed a partnership with John Wellborn Root, Jr., and the firm of Holabird & Root went on to design many buildings in Chicago and elsewhere.

He, along with his architecturally prominent son and father, is buried in a family plot at Graceland Cemetery.

The son of John Augur Holabird, John Augus Holabird, Jr., initially had thoughts of a career in theater. However, he was drawn into architecture and ultimately headed the firm that his father had cofounded. He is buried within the Holabird family plot, his site noted with a headstone bearing his name and dates.

William HOLABIRD
(1854-1923)

Graceland Cemetery,
Chicago, Illinois

Raymond HOOD
(1881-1934)

Sleepy Hollow Cemetery,
Sleepy Hollow, New York

The first in a line of what was to become an architecturally prominent family, William Holabird began by establishing a partnership with Martin Roche. The firm, Holabird & Roche, went on to design many significant building in Chicago and elsewhere. His marker is among other family members, including his architect son and grandson.

After studying at Brown University and the Massachusetts Institute of Technology, Hood received a degree from the Ecole des Beaux-Arts in Paris. His career took off when he and his partner, John Mead Howells, a fellow student at the Ecole des Beaux-Arts, won the highly publicized 1922 Tribune Tower competition in Chicago. From there the firm of Howells & Hood went on to design many high-rise buildings, including the New York Daily News and McGraw Hill Buildings in New York City.

Regrettably, Hood died just as his firm was experiencing enormous success. His unmarked burial site lies in a shallow glen covered by a lush covering of rhododendrons.

Gerald A. HORN
(1934-2014)

Port Richmond, California

IIT Campus,
Chicago, Illinois

Horn, like his mentor, Craig Ellwood, and his grand master, Mies van der Rohe, came to architecture without formal academic training. He picked up the essentials from colleagues and always showed a special sensitivity for steel design. After Ellwood closed his office and moved to rural Italy to paint, Horn moved on to Chicago to be close to Mies since he so admired the way Mies worked with steel in architecture.

Horn soon joined the Illinois Institute of Technology as a professor and it was where he taught for many years. He became a partner and chief of design for the prominent firm of Holabird & Root and added to the firm's prestige with several design awards, most notably one for the Northwestern University Law School.

After Horn's death, his ashes were divided. A portion was deposited in the waters below his steel house in Point Richmond, California. The rest were deposited beneath a plaque and a commemorative hawthorn tree planted on the campus of IIT. Appropriately, the site overlooks Crown Hall, one of his mentor's seminal buildings.

George HOWE
(1886-1955)

Mt. Auburn Cemetery,
Cambridge, Massachusetts

Howe designed several buildings in the Philadelphia area. The most important is the PSFS Building that presaged the

ARCHITECTS' GRAVESITES | 49

modern office tower, being the first International Style skyscraper in the United States. In addition, his teachings at the American Academy in Rome and at Yale University had a significant influence on other important architects, such as Louis Kahn. His marker, among those of other family members, is a simple stone tablet next to that of his wife.

John Mead HOWELLS
(1868-1959)

Cambridge Cemetery,
Cambridge, Massachusetts

Howells studied at Harvard and at the Ecole des Beaux-Arts in Paris. After several years of practice, during which he designed buildings in the art deco style, he formed a partnership with Raymond Hood, whom he had met at the Ecole des Beaux-Arts. Their firm received wide acclaim after winning the competition for the design of the Tribune Tower in Chicago. They went on to design major buildings in New York City, such as the New York Daily News Building and the McGraw-Hill Building. After Hood's death, Howells continued on, designing several major buildings.

Howells is buried within a family plot of simple stone tablets commemorating him, his wife, his namesake son and his son's wife.

Myron HUNT
(1868-1952)

San Gabriel Cemetery,
San Gabriel, California

❈ AIA Gold Medal 1967

Hunt began his career in the Chicago area and his work there showed the influence of the Prairie School that was becoming ever more popular. After receiving the commission for the design of the Rose Bowl in Pasadena, Hunt moved to California and spent the rest of his career there, designing several buildings. His simple headstone, next to that of his wife, is in a plot with a marker bearing the family name.

Richard Morris HUNT
(1827-1895)

Island Cemetery,
Newport, Rhode Island

Hunt was a profoundly influential architect in the late nineteenth century. He was the first American trained at the Ecole des Beaux-Arts in Paris. Hunt was highly regarded among his socially prominent clients, who included the Vanderbilts and the Astors. He also was a cofounder of the American Institute of Architects.

It is altogether fitting that his final resting place is in Newport, Rhode Island, the location of the summer residences of many of his wealthy clients and site of several of his important works. His plot is marked with a large polished granite ledger that bears his name, dates, and the epitaph "Laborare est orare" ("To work is to pray").

Franklin D. ISRAEL
(1945-1996)

Westwood Cemetery,
Hollywood, California

Israel was a promising architect who died prematurely before reaching his full potential. He was deeply involved in the Hollywood community, designing innovative projects for several Hollywood studios and becoming a favorite teacher at UCLA.

Appropriately his gravesite is located in a cemetery filled with Hollywood luminaries, such as Lew Ayres, Natalie Wood, and Marilyn Monroe. Israel's site is directly adjacent to that of actor Burt Lancaster.

Thomas JEFFERSON
(1743-1826)

Monticello Historic Site,
Charlottesville, Virginia

 AIA Gold Medal 1993

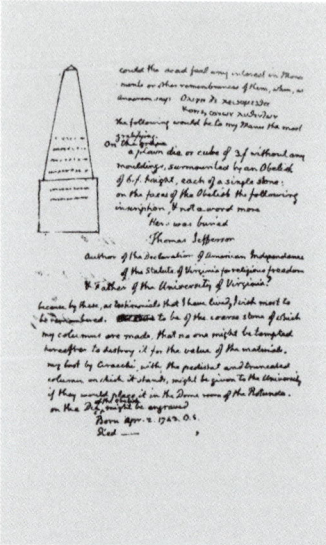

Jefferson is one of America's earliest architects and the only architect to have also been president of the United States, a truly remarkable achievement. He is also one of the rare architects who designed his own tombstone and its inscription. Though not formally trained as an architect, he designed several important structures, such as his own home, Monticello, and the main quadrangle at the University of Virginia.

It is notable that 167 years after his death the AIA awarded him their highest honor, the AIA Gold Medal.

Jefferson drew a sketch of the monument he wanted for himself. It is likely he based his design on an idea he picked up from his architect friend, Robert Mills. After Jefferson's death, his sketch was used to create a marker for him. The simple epitaph he chose for himself was "Here was buried Thomas Jefferson, author of the Declaration of American Independence, of the Statute of Virginia for religious freedom and Father of the University of Virginia"—and, he insisted, not a word more! Over the following years, souvenir seekers and vandals so damaged the monument that it was replaced with a replica in 1883, this time protected by an iron fence. The original monument was given to the University of Missouri, on whose campus it now resides.

William Le Baron JENNEY
(1832-1907)

Graceland Cemetery,
Chicago, Illinois

Jenney's Home Insurance Building in Chicago is among the first to use a metal frame rather than bearing walls to support the high-rise building's weight. Jenney was trained as an engineer and architect in Paris. He spent much of his early career on engineering projects and landscape design. He was also an early employer of Louis Sullivan, Daniel Burnham, and William Holabird.

Upon Jenney's death, his ashes were scattered in the area of his wife's grave at Graceland. Years later a monument was placed on the site. It includes a marker for Jenney that incorporates the headstone for his wife that had existed there previously. The monument includes an isometric image of a steel-framed building that commemorates Jenney's important contribution to the field of high-rise construction. Laurence Perkins is credited with the concept for the monument's design and is said to have sketched his idea on a napkin. The trustees of Graceland Cemetery commissioned architect William Bickford to turn this concept into the monument that today marks the Jenney plot.

Jens JENSEN
(1860-1951)

Memorial Gardens,
Skokie, Illinois

Jensen was a landscape designer who practiced his art throughout the Midwest. His landscaping designs were often incorporated in the projects of architects such as Albert Kahn, Howard Van Doren Shaw, and Dwight Perkins. His modest headstone includes his name along with those of his wife and children.

John JOHANSEN
(1916-2012)

Johansen studied architecture at the Harvard Graduate School of Design under Walter Gropius and, in fact, married Gropius's daughter. Johansen became associated with other modernists from the school, such as Marcel Breuer, Philip Johnson, and Eliot Noyes. He ultimately formed his own firm, which designed buildings all over the world.

Johansen was cremated and his ashes were disseminated among family members.

Philip JOHNSON
(1906-2005)

New Canaan, Connecticut

✺ AIA Gold Medal 1978

Johnson's flamboyant persona had a significant impact on the architectural world for a large part of the nearly 100 years that he lived. Born into a wealthy family, Johnson was something of a dilettante, who studied and traveled widely as a young man. He helped curate an important show at the Museum of Modern Art in New York in 1932 that introduced the International Style to the United States. That show exposed Mies van der Rohe and other International Style architects who would soon become important elements in the evolving American architecture scene. Johnson, then in his late thirties, went on to study architecture at Harvard University. From there he began his career as an architect, creating structures throughout the world.

One of Johnson's most recognized works is the Glass House, located on his estate in New Canaan. Johnson chose to have his ashes spread in his rose garden, a favorite place of his, just across the road from the Glass House. There is no marker.

A. Quincy JONES
(1913-1979)

Jones was a southern California architect and educator known for innovative design and the introduction of greenbelts into urban planning. He was the dean of architecture at the University of Southern California for several years and designed several office buildings and university buildings. He teamed up with developer Joseph Eichler in transforming typical tract housing of simple stucco boxes into an open, modern plan, usually with an atrium, and integrated into the landscape. The two of them were responsible for hundreds of modern, medium-priced houses. He also designed "Sunnyland," the much acclaimed estate of Walter Annenberg at Rancho Mirage.

Upon Jones's death his body was donated to the UCLA medical center for research, so there is no marker for his remains.

What resulted was one of America's architectural icons, the Thorncrown Chapel, the work for which he will be remembered.

It is fitting that his remains reside at the site of his most important work. His ashes were spread atop the boulder just outside the chapel beyond the altar.

E. Fay JONES
(1921-2004)

Thorncrown Chapel,
Eureka Springs, Arkansas

 AIA Gold Medal 1990

Jones taught at the University of Arkansas for most of his career. During that time he was asked to design a chapel within some nearby woodlands.

Albert KAHN
(1869-1942)

White Chapel Memorial Cemetery,
Troy, Michigan

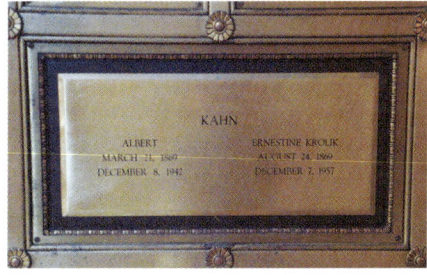

Kahn is most remembered for the many industrial buildings he designed for the automobile industry in and around Detroit. He also designed several office complexes, including the enormous General Motors Headquarters Building in Detroit. The great breadth and variety of his work prompted Frank Lloyd Wright in 1941 to consider him America's best architect at the time "because he has more work and is probably richer than any other architect."

Despite Kahn's fame and importance, his remains are quietly entombed behind a brass plaque bearing his name within the cemetery's large central mausoleum.

George Frederick (Fred) KECK
(1895-1980)

Oak Hill Cemetery,
Watertown, Wisconsin

Louis Isidore KAHN
(1901-1974)

Montefiore Cemetery,
Rockledge, Pennsylvania

❈ AIA Gold Medal 1971

Kahn's theories and his work influenced many important architects during his time. His enigmatic personality and lifestyle helped create a true mystique around the man. Although he was married, he shared prolonged relationships with two other women, one being Anne Tyng, a significant architect in her own right. His headstone, shared with his wife, resides among those of other family members.

Born in Wisconsin, Keck attended architecture school at the University of Wisconsin and the University of Illinois. He worked for several architectural firms in Chicago before starting his own firm in 1926. In 1931 his younger brother, William Keck, joined him and the firm Keck & Keck was formed.

They became early advocates of the International Style and gained recognition for their House of Tomorrow at the 1933-1934 Century of Progress in Chicago. For the same exposition they designed the all-glass Crystal House, which led them to a life-long practice of designing houses based on passive solar heating.

Keck's stone marker bears his and his wife's names and dates. His brother, William, has a similar marker nearby in the same cemetery.

Gertrude Lempp KERBIS
(1926-2016)

Graceland Cemetery,
Chicago, Illinois

Gertrude Kerbis embarked on a career in architecture after seeing an article about Frank Lloyd Wright while she was attending college. She transferred from the University of Wisconsin in Madison, which had no architectural program, to the University of Illinois in Champagne, where she earned a bachelors degree in architecture. She went on to receive masters degrees from Harvard University under Walter Gropius and from Illinois Tech (now the Illinois Institute of Technology) under Ludwig Mies van der Rohe.

She joined Skidmore, Owings & Merrill in Chicago, where she designed the innovative dining hall with its long span trusses for the United States Air Force Academy in Colorado Springs, Colorado. She brought similar innovations to the circular restaurant at O'Hare Airport in Chicago while working for Naess & Murphy. Its inverted dome roof was cable-suspended from a compression ring at the perimeter of the building. She went on to open her own office in 1968 and designed, as developer-architect, the "Greenhouse Condos" in Chicago.

She was only the eleventh woman to be made a Fellow of the American Institute of Architects (FAIA), was a founder of Chicago Women in Architecture, and was the first female president of the Chicago chapter of AIA. She also was the first woman to be president of the famed Cliff Dwellers Club in Chicago.

Her remains will be interred at Graceland Cemetery.

Fazlur KHAN
(1929-1982)

Graceland Cemetery,
Chicago, Illinois

Khan was a partner in the firm Skidmore, Owings & Merrill and was instrumental in devising structural systems for some of that firm's great triumphs, such as the Sears Tower and the John Hancock Building, both in Chicago.

Khan, a native of Bangladesh, died unexpectedly at the age of 53. He had worked closely with Bruce Graham, a managing partner at SOM, during his career, so it was this long-time friend and colleague who designed his gravesite. The site consists of a stone with an inscription written in Bengali, Khan's native tongue, and includes a saying from his native land telling of life's journey. The gravestone is surrounded by plantings of periwinkle.

The stone was raised in 2011 to be at the same level as the new marker added directly beside it, commemorating Bruce Graham. Here is an example of two architects who worked closely together and deeply admired each other having adjoining markers.

before graduating in order to pursue a concept of landscape design involving geometry and creating a series of outdoor spaces. One of his first triumphs was his collaboration with Eero Saarinen in designs for the Gateway Arch project in St. Louis, Missouri. Another was his landscape design for the J. Irwin Miller house in Columbus, Indiana. Other important projects included the United States Air Force Academy and the Oakland Museum.

Kiley spent much of his time at his rural home in Charlotte, Vermont. It is there, fittingly, that his ashes were cast near a simple marker with his name, dates, and the epitaph, "All is calm and large hearted."

Dan KILEY
(1912-2004)

Charlotte, Vermont

A pioneer in modern landscape design, Kiley left his mark with over 1,000 projects. Kiley attended the design program at Harvard University but left

Vincent George KLING
(1916-2013)

St. Peters Pikeland Church of Christ, Chester Springs, Pennsylvania

58 | ARCHITECTS' GRAVESITES

Kling studied at Columbia University and obtained a master's degree in architecture from the Massachusetts Institute of Technology. After serving as a pilot during World War II, he worked at Skidmore, Owings & Merrill before starting his own firm in Philadelphia.

He is best known for his extensive Penn Center project in New York, an assortment of high-rise office buildings and underground passageways. Having been built on the site of McKim, Mead & White's much heralded Pennsylvania Station, with its grand spaces, the Kling project drew significant criticism.

The headstone at Kling's grave bears his name and dates, as well as those of his wife.

Koch graduated from the Graduate School of Design at Harvard University.

He is best known for his prefabricated home design. His primary legacy is the Techbuilt system of prefabrication, of which over 3,000 homes were built.

Koch's love of sailing is apparent from the inclusion on his marker of a sailboat and the points of a compass as well as the tribute: architect, sailor.

Pierre KOENIG
(1925-2004)

Los Angeles National Cemetery,
Los Angeles, California

Carl KOCH
(1912-1998)

Mt. Auburn Cemetery,
Cambridge, Massachusetts

One of the influential midcentury designers working in the Los Angeles area, Koenig designed scores of houses. Two of his designs were part of the famous Case Study House Project. One of those houses, the Stahl House, received world-wide acclaim because of the iconic photograph taken by Julius Shulman, showing guests lounging in a living room cantilevered out over a vista of the Los Angeles skyline.

Koenig was born in California and attended the University of Southern California. Before striking out on his own he worked briefly with Raphael Soriano. As a veteran of World War II, he is buried austerely in a national cemetery, his marker abutting that of his father, a veteran of World War I.

Morris LAPIDUS
(1902-2001)

Lakeside Memorial Park,
Miami, Florida

Lapidus is best known for the exuberant midcentury hotels he designed in south Florida. His mammoth and opulent structures became symbols of Miami Beach during the 1950s and 1960s.

For a man so flamboyant in life, his final resting place is quite plain. His vault lies within a large, rather bland mausoleum. Remarkably, the cover plate of his space is marked only with his name and dates along with those of his wife—nothing to suggest the bigger-than-life persona of this man.

Benjamin LATROBE
(1764-1820)

St. Louis Cemetery No. 1,
New Orleans, Louisiana

Often called the father of American architecture, British-born Latrobe was the architect of the United States Capitol Building. He went on to design several more structures in Washington, D.C., and Philadelphia before moving to New Orleans, where he died of yellow fever.

Latrobe was originally buried in the Protestant section of a Catholic city cemetery. Over the years, the cemetery has been subject to massive changes and rearrangements, as a result of which the exact location of Latrobe's remains is unknown. Nevertheless, at the rear of the original cemetery are plaques that commemorate Latrobe.

John LAUTNER
(1911-1994)

Marquette, Michigan

Lautner is considered to be one of the key contemporary architects in Southern California during the 1950s and 1960s. He was raised in northern Michigan, where he attended college. In 1933, he was deeply moved by Frank Lloyd Wright's *Autobiography* and enrolled as an apprentice at Taliesin. He spent the next six years there, taking on significant responsibility for several of Wright's projects, such as the Millard House in Los Angeles, "Wingspread" in Racine, Wisconsin, and the Willey House in Minneapolis. Lautner then moved to California to set up his own architectural practice but continued to assist with several of Wright's California projects.

Lautner's architectural style utilized progressive engineering concepts that he applied with flair. His time with Wright caused his designs to embody organic elements, as well. Of the over 200 buildings that he designed during his career, most of his best-known work was residential. Many of these projects were built on steep, difficult sites where he would take advantage of the magnificent views by creating dramatic structures.

After Lautner's death, his ashes were cast at the family home in northern Michigan, "Midgaard," which his parents designed and he helped build when he was a child.

LE CORBUSIER
(Charles Eduard Jeanneret)
(1887-1965)

Roqubrune, Cap Martin, France

 AIA Gold Medal 1961

Even though he never resided in the United States and his work here was limited, Le Corbusier had an enormous impact on American architecture. He is considered one of the pioneers of the modern movement in architecture and his influence on other architects was profound. His only work in the United States, other than his being a consultant on the United Nations Secretariat Building in New York, is the Carpenter Center on the Harvard University campus in Cambridge, Massachusetts. Regrettably, his concept of tall residential towers built atop expansive park-like spaces, so beautifully executed in his Unite d'habitation in Marsailles, France, became the prototype for many large, and virtually unlivable, public housing projects built across the United States during the 1950s and 1960s.

He is one of the few architects who actually designed his own grave marker, which he did after the death of his wife in 1957. He died eight years later while on one of his frequent swims in the Mediterranean.

His marker stands upon a stone pad overlooking the Mediterranean. Next to an urn is a small structure that houses colorful plaques for his wife and him.

Ricardo LEGORRETA
(1931-2011)

Panteon Frances de San Joaquin, Mexico City, Mexico

✺ AIA Gold Medal 2000

While never living in the United States, Legorreta, like Le Corbusier, had a profound impact on architectural development in America. Legorreta introduced Mexican modernism to a global audience and brought his crisp, brightly colored aesthetic to the American Southwest. His work featured the clean lines and spare forms of modern design while incorporating elements of Mexican vernacular architecture, such as protective walls, spacious courtyards, and bold colors.

He is perhaps best known for his Camino Real Hotel in Mexico City (1965) and his purple tower in Pershing Square, Los Angeles (1994). More recently he designed a large dormitory complex, the Max Palevsky Commons (2001), at the University of Chicago. Here his bold colors and stark shapes stand apart from the somber Collegiate Gothic-style buildings that surround it. The relative liveliness of his project has made it a favorite of the undergraduates who live there.

His remains are buried in a niche within a large family mausoleum. He is remembered with a small plaque bearing his name and dates.

Pierre L'ENFANT
(1754-1852)

Arlington National Cemetery, Arlington, Virginia

French-born L'Enfant, an architect and civil engineer, left France to fight with the Americans during the Revolutionary War. He remained in the United States after the war and established himself in New York City, designing several projects. He later moved on to Washington, D.C., where he was hired to develop a master plan for the city.

L'Enfant has perhaps the most dramatic and appropriate burial site of any architect. His ceremonial ledger sits beneath a classical table on a crest overlooking a breathtaking panoramic view of the city that he designed.

William E. LESCAZE
(1896-1969)

Kensico Cemetery,
Valhalla, New York

Lescaze was born in Switzerland and studied there under Karl Moser before coming to the United States. He is best known for the PSFS Building (1932) in Philadelphia, which he did in partnership with George Howe. This building is considered to be the first American skyscraper in the International Style. He also designed a new building for MoMA that was never built. He went on to teach at the Pratt Institute and was a pioneer in the design of modern urban townhouses, many of which were built in New York City and Brooklyn.

Lescaze's grave is marked with a tablet bearing his and his wife's names and dates.

Jerrold LOEBL
(1899-1978)

Rosehill Cemetery,
Chicago, Illinois

Loebl was a partner in the firm of Loebl Schlossman in Chicago, which designed several important projects, including the Old Orchard Shopping Center, one of the first postwar malls in the Chicago area. His remains reside behind a marble panel in the cemetery's central mausoleum.

Anthony J. LUMSDEN
(1928-2011)

Lumsden was born in England and raised in Australia, where he studied architecture. After traveling in Europe he came to the United States and worked in the office of Eero Saarinen.

After Saarinen's death Lumsden continued working for the Roche Dinkeloo firm. In 1965, he and a colleague, Cesar Pelli, left for California to work for Daniel, Mann, Johnson & Mendenhall, where Lumsden soon became the design principal and was responsible for several award-winning designs.

His ashes are held by a family member.

is buried next to him. The son's gravesite is marked with an urn that seems to upstage the simple markers of his parents.

George Washington MAHER
(1864-1926)

Rosehill Cemetery,
Chicago, Illinois

Marion MAHONY (Griffin)
(1871-1961)

Graceland Cemetery,
Chicago, Illinois

Maher is known for the many homes that he designed, primarily in the Chicago area. His career was at its peak when the Prairie Style was developing, so his buildings incorporate many elements of that style while at the same time displaying his unique characteristics, such as monumental central entrances and exaggerated proportions.

Maher committed suicide at the age of 62 and his burial site is marked with a simple headstone, next to that of his wife. His son, Philip Brooks Maher, also an architect of several notable buildings,

Mahony was one of the first women to receive an architectural degree. Her early work was in the office of Frank Lloyd Wright where, among other things, she delineated many of the drawings for the ultimate publishing of Wright's work by Wasmuth in Germany. It was at Wright's office that she met another emerging architect, Walter Burley Griffin. They married and moved to Australia when their entry had won the competition to design that country's capital city, Canberra. After several years in Australia, the two moved to India, where Griffin was involved with several projects. After the death of Griffin, Mahony returned to the United States and took up residence with a

ARCHITECTS' GRAVESITES | 65

relative in Chicago. She did little architectural work but wrote a lengthy memoir, *The Magic of America.*

After her death, her ashes were buried near a family member's remains in Graceland Cemetery but without any marker. In 1997, through the efforts of a Graceland trustee, John Notz, Mahony's remains were moved to a burial spot in the cemetery's new columbarium. The site is marked by a plaque designed by John Eifler, which incorporates flowers drawn by Mahony in the sketch she did for Wright for the Hardy House in Racine, Wisconsin.

Benjamin MARSHALL
(1874-1940)

Rosehill Cemetery,
Chicago, Illinois

Marshall is best known for the many hotels and large apartment houses that he designed, primarily in the Chicago area. His remains reside within a large, rather plain family mausoleum.

Bernard MAYBECK
(1862-1957)

Mountain View Cemetery,
Piedmont, California

✽ AIA Gold Medal 1951

After studying architecture at the Ecole des Beaux-Arts in Paris, Maybeck took up residence in California, where he became a professor at the University of California at Berkeley. It was there that he influenced a generation of developing architectural talent. He designed in a wide range of architectural styles but is best remembered for his works in the Mission Style. His simple bronze marker resides within a large and peaceful courtyard.

Charles McKIM
(1847-1909)

Rosedale Cemetery,
Orange, New Jersey

❊ AIA Gold Medal 1907

McKim was born in Pennsylvania and attended Harvard University and the Ecole des Beaux-Arts in Paris. He worked as a draftsman for Henry Hobson Richardson on the Trinity Church project in Boston, Massachusetts. In 1879 he joined with William Mead and Stanford White to form the firm McKim, Mead & White, one of the most successful and influential firms in the country. Their early work included several Shingle Style residences in the Newport, Rhode Island, area. Later work embodied Italian Renaissance and classical motifs in such projects as Pennsylvania Station and the University Club in New York and the Boston Public Library. During the 1893 Columbian Exposition in Chicago, he and Daniel Burnham developed a close personal and professional relationship that continued until McKim's death.

He is buried within a family plot that has a low perimeter wall of stone panels, each inscribed with the name of a family member, including McKim himself.

Montgomery MEIGS
(1816-1905)

Arlington National Cemetery,
Arlington, Virginia

Meigs was a brigadier general in the U.S. Army, an engineer, and an architect, who is noted for his many engineering feats during the Civil War as well as for the buildings he designed.

His marker is a large sarcophagus that lists his many accomplishments. Directly adjacent to his marker is a plaintive bronze sculpture of his oldest son, Lt. John Rogers Meigs, which shows him lying dead with a pistol by his side. Lt. Meigs, having graduated first in his class at West Point, fought in the Civil War and was appointed chief engineer under General Philip Sheridan. On maneuvers one evening Meigs encountered some rebel soldiers. A fight broke out, and he was killed. His father, wishing to avenge his son's death, offered a large reward to find his son's murderer. Lt. Meigs's marker, depicting his death scene, indicates the grief that his father must have felt.

Erich MENDELSOHN
(1887-1953)

San Francisco, California

Born in Germany, Mendelsohn soon rose as a promising architectural talent among other such as Mies van der Rohe and Gropius. During this time he designed several significant structures, including the remarkable expressionist Einstein Tower. As a Jew, Mendelsohn faced increasing anti-Semitism and in 1933 fled to England. After his departure, the Germans confiscated the assets he had left behind and struck his name from all architecture records. During his years in England, Mendelsohn designed many buildings, a significant portion of them in Palestine.

In 1941, he moved to the United States and settled in California's Bay Area. He taught for many years at the Berkeley campus of the University of California. His fame as an architect after he moved to the United States never reached the levels that he had achieved during his early years in Germany. He resided in San Francisco, where he devoted most of his design talents to projects for the Jewish community. He asked that after his death his ashes be scattered upon the waters of San Francisco Bay.

Ludwig MIES VAN DER ROHE
(1886-1969)

Graceland Cemetery, Chicago, Illinois

AIA Gold Medal 1960

Mies van der Rohe is considered by many to be one of the most important American architects of the mid- to late twentieth century. He was acknowledged throughout the world and a commemorative postage was issued in his honor by the United States Postal Service.

His career began in Germany, where he designed several important buildings, including the Barcelona Pavilion (1929) and the Tugendhat House (1930). Mies migrated to the United States in the 1930s and took up residence in Chicago, where he taught at the Illinois Institute of Technology and practiced architecture. During this time he created many seminal buildings, including Crown Hall at the Illinois Institute of Technology, the apartment buildings on Lake Shore Drive in Chicago, and the Farnsworth House in Plano, Illinois, along with several buildings abroad. Mies's principle of "less is more" dominated the development of modern architecture, and his influence on other architects was profound.

Mies is buried beneath a honed granite slab designed by his architect grandson, Dirk Lohan. The understated yet elegant nature of the marker perfectly personifies the architect who is buried here.

Robert MILLS
(1781-1855)

Congressional Cemetery, Washington, D.C.

One of America's first architects, Mills is best known as the designer of the Washington Memorial in Washington, D.C. His grave is marked with a tall marble tablet that calls out his many accomplishments.

Mockbee became known as "the citizen architect" and his work was acknowledged by awards from both the Graham and the MacArthur Foundations.

Mockbee is buried beneath a conventional stone tablet making note of his name, dates, and military service.

Samuel N. MOCKBEE
(1944-2001)

Magnolia Cemetery,
Meridian, Mississippi

✽ AIA Gold Medal 2004

Growing up in Mississippi and spending much of his life in the Deep South of the United States, Mockbee ultimately committed his efforts toward providing safe, well-constructed, and inspirational housing for the large number of disadvantaged rural inhabitants to which he had been exposed. He taught at Auburn University and often had students design structures using what would otherwise have been discarded materials. As a result of his efforts,

László MOHOLY-NAGY
(1895-1946)

Graceland Cemetery,
Chicago, Illinois

Born in Hungary, Moholy-Nagy was an instructor at the Bauhaus in Germany until its Nazi-compelled closing in the mid-1930s. He moved to England and then to the United States. He opened his own school of design in Chicago in 1939 and devoted the

rest of his career to the school and to his own painting and photography work. A few years after his death, the school became a department of the Illinois Institute of Technology. Moholy-Nagy's cremated remains lie beneath a small stone marker.

Charles Willard MOORE
(1925-1993)

Cemetario el Encinal,
Monterey, California

 AIA Gold Medal 1991

After receiving a Ph.D. in architecture at Princeton, Moore continued on there as a teacher, assisting Louis Kahn. He moved to the University of California at Berkeley to teach for a short time before returning east to become dean at the Yale School of Architecture in 1965. He ultimately ended up in Austin, Texas, as a professor at the University of Texas.

Besides being an educator and a prolific writer, Moore is known for his vigorous architectural designs, often using bold colors, shapes, and materials. He, along with Robert Venturi and Michael Graves, is considered one of the pioneers in postmodern architecture—a strong counterpoint to the rigidity and starkness of the modernist style.

Unique among all of his architectural brethren, Moore has the distinction of having his ashes encrypted next to those of his mother, with a simple stone plaque noting them both.

Julia MORGAN
(1872-1957)

Mountain View Cemetery,
Piedmont, California

 AIA Gold Medal 2014

Morgan graduated with a civil engineering degree from the University of California and went on to be the first woman to study architecture at the Ecole de Beaux-Arts in Paris. During her career she designed many structures, including the castle at San Simeon, home of William Randolph Hearst, the publishing tycoon.

Despite her many achievements as an architect, her name is included, rather plainly, among those of other family members on a simple stone marker. Many years after her death the AIA acknowledged her importance and bestowed its AIA Gold Medal award on her, the first time it had ever been awarded to a woman.

firms after graduation. He became a partner in the firm Dubin, Dubin & Moutoussamy, where he eventually became managing partner.

He was vice chairman of the Chicago Plan Commission and was a trustee of the Art Institute of Chicago. He designed several junior colleges in Chicago and is best known for the office building he designed for *Jet* magazine.

His grave is marked with a simple headstone.

John W. MOUTOUSSAMY
(1922-1995)

St. Mary Cemetery,
Evergreen Park, Illinois

Charles F. MURPHY, SR.
(1890-1985)

Calvary Cemetery,
Evanston, Illinois

Moutoussamy was a prominent Chicago-area African American architect. He studied architecture under Mies van der Rohe at the Illinois Institute of Technology and worked for Chicago-area

Having served as personal secretary to Ernest Graham at the firm of Graham, Anderson, Probst & White, Murphy was discharged upon Graham's death. He soon established a firm of his own that ultimately became C. F. Murphy Associates. The firm went on to design some of Chicago's most significant buildings—McCormick Place, O'Hare Airport, the First National Bank Building, and the Daley Center. The firm also became a haven for talented young architects who would go on to distinguished careers, such as Gene Summers, Helmut Jahn, and John Burgee.

Murphy was also the executor of the Ernest Graham estate. He used those funds to establish the Graham Foundation for Advanced Study in the Fine Arts. Under Murphy's guidance, the Graham Foundation assets grew and the foundation became a leader in the field of architectural study and philanthropy.

Murphy's grave is marked with a simple headstone citing both him and his wife.

Walter NETSCH
(1920-2008)

Graceland Cemetery,
Chicago, Illinois

Netsch was a partner in the Chicago office of Skidmore, Owings & Merrill. Included in his list of projects are the Air Force Academy Chapel, the Chicago campus of the University of Illinois, and Regenstein Library at the University of Chicago.

Unlike most of the other architects explored in this study, Netsch and his wife made detailed plans for their gravesite prior to his death. He and his wife, Dawn Clark Netsch, a former Illinois state senator and state comptroller, chose their site and on it they planted a ginkgo tree, a favorite of both of them. This particular tree was chosen because its two forked branches represent the Netsches' two independent careers. The monument was designed by Wayne Tjaden, an associate of Netsch, and includes complex symbolism that relates to Netsch's views of design.

Richard NEUTRA
(1892-1970)

Silver Lake, California

❀ AIA Gold Medal 1977

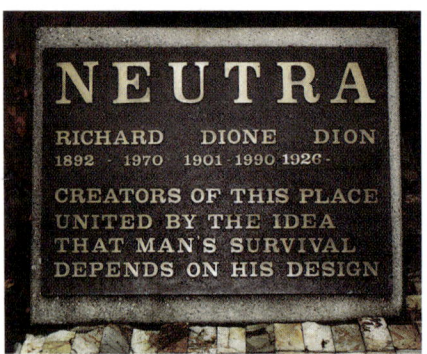

An immigrant from Austria, Neutra worked for a time with Frank Lloyd Wright and Rudolph Schindler. Neutra developed into a leading modernist and designed several residences in southern California, the most famous being the Kaufmann and Lovell Houses.

Neutra's cremated remains reside in a garden beside the house that he designed for himself. The site is marked with a bronze plaque.

Matthew (Maciej) NOWICKI
(1910-1950)

Civil International Cemetery, Cairo, Egypt

Warsaw, Poland

Matthew Nowicki has been referred to as a forgotten genius. Lewis Mumford said that had he not died so early in his career, at the age of forty, he might have become the greatest architect of our time. Eero Saarinen described him as being one of the great influences in his life.

Born in Chita, Russia, Nowicki began his career in Poland, where he designed the Polish pavilion at the 1939 New York World's Fair. He also worked on plans for the reconstruction of Warsaw following World War II. He moved to New York City in 1945 as an official delegate of the Polish government. He found himself stranded in the United States when Poland fell under the control of the Communist party. He affiliated with what is now North Carolina State University, where he became acting head of the newly formed school of architecture. It was there that he began to spread his architectural wings as he developed a style that incorporated bold engineering concepts into his designs. At North Carolina State University, he designed the widely publicized J. S. Dorton Arena (completed after his death) that incorporated two dramatically sloping parabolic arches. Later he worked with Eero Saarinen on a campus master plan for Brandeis University. It is speculated that Saarinen used the Dorton Arena as an inspiration for his TWA terminal in New York and his Ingalls Hockey Rink in New Haven, Connecticut.

Ultimately, Nowicki was appointed chief architect of the new Indian capital city of Chandigarh, a project that was completed by Le Corbusier after Nowicki's death, and which gained the French architect worldwide recognition. Nowicki was returning from the Indian project when his plane crashed near Cairo, killing all of the occupants. Reportedly there is a marker at the site of the crash that notes, simply, "architect."

There was also a small memorial added to his parents' grave in Warsaw.

Eliot F. NOYES
(1910-1977)

Chilmark Cemetery,
Martha's Vineyard, Massachusetts

Noyes was an architect and industrial designer who designed everything from office buildings to the IBM Selectric typewriter. Noyes is buried on his beloved Martha's Vineyard in a cemetery overlooking the sea. His sudden death caused his family the unexpected challenge of providing a fitting monument for him. The family went to a design colleague of Noyes who, with a local stonecutter, created the modest black slate slab that bears his name.

Frederick Law OLMSTED
(1822-1903)

Old North Cemetery,
Hartford, Connecticut

Olmsted's name is synonymous with late nineteenth century landscape design throughout the country—from Central Park in New York City to the great Columbian Exposition of 1893 in Chicago.

His grave is in a large underground vault devoted to the Olmsted family. Regrettably, the cemetery is located in a deteriorating part of Hartford and has suffered from neglect and vandalism. Where once ornate gates marked the entrance to the Olmsted vault, now steel plates ominously protect the site.

Also buried here is his son, Frederick Law Olmsted, Jr. (1870-1957), a significant landscape designer in his own right.

His gravesite is at the tip of a cliff overlooking the Pacific Ocean on a site that includes his beloved home, Wild Bird. A boulder on the site bears the inscription "Instinct, untrammeled and free." His wife's ashes also reside there. This site is perhaps the most dramatic, and most inaccessible, of any architect studied in this project.

Nathaniel OWINGS
(1903-1984)

Big Sur, California

 AIA Gold Medal 1983

Owings was a founding partner of the architectural firm of Skidmore, Owings & Merrill. He more than anyone else was the public face of the firm. He became deeply involved in the arts and in several redesign concepts for Washington, D.C.

Robert S. PEABODY
(1845-1917)

Mt. Auburn Cemetery, Cambridge, Massachusetts

Peabody was raised in Massachusetts and attended Harvard University and the Ecole des Beaux-Arts in Paris. With John Stearns (1843-1917), Peabody & Stearns was formed, one of the premier architectural firms in the United States in the late nineteenth and early twentieth centuries. They designed the colossal Machinery Hall Building for Chicago's Columbian Exposition of 1893 and the Boston Custom House Tower (1915), Boston's tallest building for many years.

Peabody's grave is marked with a large stone cross bearing his name and dates.

William Leonard PEREIRA
(1909-1985)

Santa Monica Bay, California

Pereira began his career in his hometown of Chicago, where he helped draft the master plan for the 1933-1934 Century of Progress exhibition. He then moved to Los Angeles, where he became involved with the movie industry, serving as art director and production designer on several films.

It was in Los Angeles that his architectural career took off, leading to the design of over 400 buildings and projects. His designs were often futuristic and highly distinctive, embodying strong geometric shapes. In partnership with Charles Luckman, the firm of Pereira & Luckman became one of the largest in the country. One of Pereira's designs, the Transamerica (Pyramid) Building in San Francisco, California, has become an icon in that city's skyline. Another of his distinctive designs is the Theme Building at the Los Angeles International Airport, with its bold sweeping arches that support what was to be a revolving restaurant.

Upon his death, Pereira wanted there to be no service of any kind. An avid sailor, he asked that his ashes be taken out to sea and scattered over Santa Monica Bay.

Dwight PERKINS
(1867-1941)

Graceland Cemetery, Chicago, Illinois

Dwight Perkins was an influential architect at the turn of the twentieth century and an elder among a group of architects that had offices in Chicago's Steinway Hall. This group included such rising stars as Frank Lloyd Wright, the Pond brothers, Walter Burley Griffin, and Howard Van Doren Shaw. Perkins designed several schools while chief architect for the Chicago school board, as well as many residences.

He is buried in the Perkins family plot at Graceland Cemetery. Each family member's grave is marked with a headstone of identical design. His headstone includes his name as well as that of his wife, Lucy Fitch, a noted illustrator and author of children's books.

Lawrence Perkins followed in his father's architectural footsteps and, with partner Philip Will, formed the firm of Perkins & Will in Chicago, which designed scores of major office buildings and educational facilities.

Larry Perkins is buried in the Perkins family plot, nearby his famous architect father, Dwight Perkins. His headstone, bearing his and his wife's names and dates, is in the same style as that of the other family markers.

Lawrence PERKINS
(1907-1997)

Graceland Cemetery, Chicago, Illinois

Charles PLATT
(1861-1933)

South Manchester, Connecticut

Born in New York City, Platt initially aspired to become an artist. He studied painting in New York and later in Paris. Along the way he became interested in landscape design. His skills as an artist and his exploration of landscape design became known among the East Coast's aristocratic families. He soon was commissioned to design country estates for such clients as Edith Rockefeller McCormick and Vincent Astor, a townhome for Sara Delano Roosevelt, and several projects for H. Wendell Endicott. Other projects include the Greer Gallery in Washington, D.C., and the campus of the University of Illinois in Urbana.

Platt's remains reside in the family plot of his mother's family, the Cheneys.

Allen POND
(1858-1929)
and Irving POND
(1857-1939)

Forest Hill Cemetery,
Ann Arbor, Michigan

These two brother architects spent most of their careers in partnership, designing many residences throughout the Midwest. It was their desire that, upon their deaths, they would be cremated and returned to their family plot in Ann Arbor. Their markers are simple side-by-side headstones, similar to those of nearby family members.

John Russell POPE
(1874-1937)

Berkeley Memorial Cemetery,
Middletown, Rhode Island

Pope, a classically trained architect, is best known for his design of the Jefferson Memorial in Washington, D.C. His grave is located in a family plot within a small country cemetery. His headstone shares the same design as those of several relatives nearby.

George POST
(1837-1913)

Woodlawn Cemetery,
Bronx, New York

✤ AIA Gold Medal 1911

Post designed many of the early skyscrapers in New York City as well as mansions for such prestigious families as the Vanderbilts and the Huntingtons. Post's ledger lies in front of an obelisk bearing the family name.

William Gray PURCELL
(1880-1965)

Waldheim Cemetery,
Forest Park, Illinois

Purcell spent much of his career in partnership with George Elmslie designing Prairie Style residences throughout the Midwest. His burial site is marked by a pylon bearing his name and dates, using a stylized art deco font.

Adjacent to the pylon are headstones for both Purcell and his wife, Cecily. These intimate markers, bearing their signatures and dates, nearly touch at the point at which the year of their wedding is carved into the two stones.

Eleanor RAYMOND
(1887-1989)

Mt. Auburn Cemetery, Cambridge, Massachusetts

Ralph RAPSON
(1914-2008)

Lakewood Cemetery, Minneapolis, Minnesota

After working with Eero Saarinen early in his career, Rapson moved to Minnesota, where he taught and practiced architecture. His brutalist monument, reminiscent of the style he used in many of his designs, is indeed a bold and somewhat overwhelming statement. It was designed by Rapson himself for his wife, who preceded him in death. Upon his death, his ashes were scattered at the site.

After graduation from Wellesley College, Raymond did graduate work at the Cambridge School. Upon graduation she became a partner of Henry Frost, one of the founders of the Cambridge School and an architecture professor at Harvard University.

Raymond designed one of the first houses in the International Style in the United States as well as an early solar house. Her work was mostly residential and was always tempered by respect for early American architecture.

She is buried beneath a stylishly designed tablet that shows her name and dates.

ARCHITECTS' GRAVESITES | 81

Andrew N. REBORI
(1886-1966)

New Orleans, Louisiana

Rebori studied for two years at the Massachusetts Institute of Technology and the Ecole des Beaux-Arts in Paris before receiving his degree in architecture from Armour Tech (now IIT) in Chicago. He continued to teach at that institution for several years while designing a number of remarkable buildings, such as the chapel at Loyola University and the Frank Fisher Studio Apartments, both in Chicago. He is also known for creating the "Streets of Paris" exhibition at the Chicago Century of Progress exhibition of 1933-1934, which featured fan dancer Sally Rand and the bawdy shows from the Latin Quarter in New Orleans.

His ashes were deposited in the Mississippi River at New Orleans, Louisiana.

James RENWICK
(1819-1895)

Green-Wood Cemetery, Brooklyn, New York

Renwick was an important early architect who designed, among other things, St. Patrick's Cathedral in New York City. His monument, a blunt pylon, notes that he was an architect.

Henry Hobson RICHARDSON
(1838-1886)

Walnut Hills Cemetery, Brookline, Massachusetts

Richardson was a highly influential architect in the late nineteenth century, creating a style that became known as Richardsonian Romanesque. He was born in Louisiana and went on to study at Tulane University and Harvard University. His initial interest in civil engineering shifted to architecture, and he continued his studies at the Ecole des Beaux-Arts in Paris. Following Richard Morris Hunt, he was the second American to attend that prestigious institution. Because of his family's financial difficulties brought on by the Civil War, he was unable to complete his studies there and returned to the United States in 1865.

As he began his practice of architecture, he abandoned the classical style that was taught at the Ecole and, instead, began working with the Romanesque style that he had encountered in southern France. In 1869, he received the commission for the Buffalo State Asylum for the Insane, which was the largest commission of his career and the introduction of his Richardson Romanesque style. From his success with that commission, he went on to design other major buildings, including Trinity Church in Boston, the New York State Capitol Building in Albany, New York, the Allegheny County Court House in Pittsburgh, Pennsylvania, and the Marshall Field Wholesale Store in Chicago, Illinois.

Richardson died abruptly at the age of forty-seven. He is buried in a family plot in a cemetery near where he lived most of his life. Beneath a protective canopy of tree branches, his ledger, along with the markers for other family members, lies in quiet repose.

Theodate Pope RIDDLE
(1868-1946)

Riverside Cemetery,
Farmington, Connecticut

Born as Effie Brooks Pope, her father was a wealthy Ohio industrialist. Early in her life she early on changed her name to Theodate in memory of her grandmother. She was a cousin of architect Philip Johnson's mother, Louisa Pope, who also named Philip's younger sister, Theodate, in honor of the grandmother. Riddle had the harrowing experience in 1915 of surviving the sinking of the Lusitania.

Riddle took up architecture with private tutoring from two architects in Charles McKim's office and became the first licensed female architect in New York and Connecticut. Her best-known works are the Avon Old Farms School for Boys, which she founded and financed, the Westover School, and Hill-Stead, the family home in Farmington, Connecticut, which is now a public museum of the family's art collection.

She is buried beneath a stone ledger that bears her name and dates.

Hilyard ROBINSON
(1899-1986)

National Harmony Memorial Park,
Landover, Maryland

Robinson was one of the most successful and productive African American architects in Washington, D.C., during the first half of the twentieth century. He helped address the housing needs of blacks from poor to affluent.

He was a key figure in spurring public housing legislation in the 1930s and received the first commission from the new Public Works Administration (PWA) for Langston Terrace in

Washington, D.C. He was well prepared for the task, having earned both BA and MA architectural degrees from Columbia University. He also studied with Paul Cret at the University of Pennsylvania and spent time in Europe studying public housing, as well.

He taught for several years at Howard University, heading its architecture department and designing several buildings for the university.

He is buried beneath a bronze plaque that calls out his service in World War I.

Martin ROCHE
(1853-1927)

Calvary Cemetery,
Evanston, Illinois

Roche was a partner with William Holabird in the firm of Holabird & Roche. Their firm designed many high-rise office towers. His gravesite is marked with a monument bearing only the family name. There are no individual markers for him or any of the family members that are buried here.

John ROEBLING
(1800-1869)

Riverview Cemetery,
Trenton, New Jersey

Roebling was one of the pioneers in large construction projects, including several record-setting suspension bridges—culminating in the Brooklyn Bridge. During the early days of construction of that bridge, Roebling was injured in a ferryboat accident and died before seeing his greatest work completed.

Roebling is buried in a family plot marked with a large monument bearing the family name. Headstones for him and other family members lie before it. On his marker he is noted simply as a "civil engineer."

Washington ROEBLING
(1837-1926)

Cold Spring Cemetery,
Cold Spring, New York

Washington Roebling, trained as an engineer like his father, John Roebling, took over leadership of the Brooklyn Bridge project after his father's death. He became deeply involved with that project, even spending time in the caissons that were used in building the bases of the two gigantic towers. It was his exposure to that environment that caused him to become ill with caissons disease, which is similar to "the bends" suffered by underwater divers.

As a result, he was confined to his home for the remainder of the construction of the Brooklyn Bridge, having to rely on watching the project through a telescope from his home in Brooklyn Heights. His only contact with the construction site was by way of his wife, untrained as an engineer, who would act as the intermediary between her husband and construction managers on the job site. He said that the bridge could not have been completed without his wife's involvement.

Fittingly, both Washington Roebling and his wife, Emily Roebling, are buried beneath twin monuments of equal stature. Both monuments are within a large circular stone coping.

James Gamble ROGERS
(1867-1947)

Born in Kentucky, Rogers attended Yale University. He soon was befriended by benefactor Edward Harkness and became his favorite architect. This led to several commissions at Yale and elsewhere where Harkness's gift was conditional upon Rogers being used as the architect. Rogers work at Yale was extensive and included such projects as Harkness Tower, the centerpiece of the Yale campus, the Sterling Law Building, the Hall of Graduate Studies, and several of the new residential colleges. Elsewhere Rogers designed major projects, such as the Yale Club, Columbia Presbyterian Hospital, and the Memorial Sloan-Kettering Hospital, all in New York City.

Rogers designed his buildings in the Collegiate Gothic style in which he borrowed styles from university buildings in places such as Oxford and Cambridge in England. His throwback architectural style was criticized by those at the time who were taken with the modernist movement that was then emerging. It is interesting to note, however, that architect Robert A. M. Stern has chosen one of Roger's designed colleges (Jonathan Edwards College [1932]) at Yale as his model for the two new colleges he is designing at that university.

The location of Roger's remains are unknown. There is a memorial plaque in his honor at the base of the Harkness Tower he designed at Yale.

John Wellborn ROOT
(1850-1891)

Graceland Cemetery,
Chicago Illinois

Root was the partner of Daniel Burnham in the firm of Burnham & Root. In their short practice together their firm designed several residences and office buildings. During preparations for the 1893 Columbian Exposition, for which Root would probably have played an influential role in the overall architectural look of the project, Root contracted pneumonia and died abruptly. Burnham was with Root when he died and said that he did not know how he could go on without Root by his side.

Root is buried in a plot at Graceland that had been owned by Daniel Burnham. The central marker, designed by the Burnham & Root office, is a Celtic cross signifying Root's Scottish heritage and a form he deeply admired. One of the panels on the cross has been replaced with an elevation scheme for the Phoenix Building, which he was designing at the time of his death. Thus, on this architect's marker is captured one of his own designs. Root's actual burial site is marked with a simple red granite headstone.

ARCHITECTS' GRAVESITES | 87

John Wellborn ROOT, JR.
(1887-1963)

Graceland Cemetery,
Chicago, Illinois

❋ AIA Gold Medal 1958

Sharing the name of his famous architect father, Root studied architecture in Paris. While there he befriended another son of a famous Chicago architect, John Augur Holabird. The two returned to Chicago and joined the firm of Holabird & Roche. After several years the firm eventually became Holabird & Root and went on to design several notable art deco structures, such as the Chicago Board of Trade Building and the Chicago Daily News Building.

Root's grave bears a marker made of the same red granite and the same dimensions as that of his father, who lies nearby. The only difference is the use of a more modern font and the designation of "architect."

Arthur ROTCH
(1850-1894)

Mt. Auburn Cemetery,
Cambridge, Massachusetts

Rotch studied at Harvard University, the Massachusetts Institute of Technology, and the Ecole des Beaux-Arts. He is best known for having created, with his brother and sisters, the Rotch Traveling Scholarship in honor of their father. The scholarship is administered by the Boston Society of Architects and carries a generous stipend for travel abroad. Several recipients, such as Henry Bacon, Ralph Walker, Wallace Harrison, Louis Skidmore, and Edward Stone, have gone on to be awarded the AIA Gold Medal. They join several others, such as Gordon Bunshaft and Victor Lundy, who also had significant careers in architecture. The Rotch Library for architecture and planning at MIT is named for him.

Rotch's marker is a pointed stone tablet resting upon a ledger.

Paul RUDOLPH
(1918-1997)

New Haven, Connecticut

Rudolph was an architect of significant influence who headed the Yale School of Architecture. He designed a number of buildings, many of which were in the brutalist style, which he helped foster. That style has since fallen into disfavor and, along with it, much of the attention devoted to Rudolph has diminished. His important buildings include the Arts and Architecture Building at Yale and the Lippo Building in Hong Kong.

Upon his death, his ashes were scattered in several places. Knowledgeable sources suggest that a portion was deposited within the ventilating system of his Arts and Architecture Building. Thus, he seems to have achieved a lasting presence in this building that has been so strongly associated with his success and fall from grace. Ironically, the building has since been renamed Rudolph Hall.

Charles RUTAN
(1851-1914)

Walnut Hills Cemetery, Brookline, Massachusetts

Rutan was a partner in the firm of Shepley, Rutan & Coolidge, which succeeded the firm of H. H. Richardson after Richardson's death. He is buried in the same cemetery as Richardson, at a site marked with a headstone topped with a large cross.

Eero SAARINEN
(1910-1961)

White Chapel Memorial Cemetery, Troy, Michigan

❀ AIA Gold Medal 1962

Eero Saarinen, the son of Finnish architect Eliel Saarinen, moved to the United States with his family as a young man. He attended Yale University and practiced architecture at the Cranbrook Academy with his father until his father's death. While there he collaborated with Charles Eames on several design projects. Eames, along with his father and Matthew Nowicki, he said were to biggest influences in his professional life.

During the next ten years of his career, his firm designed dozens of major buildings throughout the world. At the height of his career, he died abruptly of a brain tumor.

Owing to the suddenness of his illness and death, there had been no forethought regarding his burial arrangements. The cemetery was selected because of its closeness to where he worked and lived. His burial site seems lost in a vast open space among hundreds of other markers for unrelated people. Once his marker is located, it is distinguished by its utter simplicity and grace; it is made of cast metal rather than the more common stone of the surrounding monuments. Next to Saarinen's marker is a similar marker for his second wife, Aline, a noted television journalist and critic. After their marriage, she spearheaded the marketing effort for Saarinen's firm—she being perhaps the first marketing executive in any architectural firm. It is believed that she designed the two markers.

Eliel SAARINEN
(1873-1950)

Hivittrack, Helsinki, Finland

❀ AIA Gold Medal 1947

Eliel Saarinen was an established and well-recognized architect when he moved from Finland to the United States in the 1920s. He helped establish the Cranbrook Academy in Michigan, which served as his base of operations until his death. He was awarded the AIA Gold Medal in 1947. Fifteen years later his son received the same award, making them the only father and son to have won this high honor.

It was at Cranbrook that his design concepts had profound impact, not only on his son Eero, but also on a raft of other young designers such as Charles Eames, Harry Weese, and Ralph Rapson.

Saarinen is buried on the expansive grounds of his family's home outside of Helsinki. Down a trail from the house, one finds a large, circular concave stone with an inscription etched into it: "Work is the key to creative growth of the mind." Nearby is a headstone with his and his wife's names.

Rudolph SCHINDLER
(1887-1953)

Silver Lake, California

A close friend and associate of Richard Neutra, Schindler also spent most of his design years in southern California, designing houses that advanced the modernist movement. One of his most important designs is the Lovell Beach House in Newport Beach.

Like those of his friend Neutra, Schindler's ashes reside in Silver Lake, California, at a house that he designed. However, in Schindler's case, his ashes were put away in a crawl space within the house and were never found when the house was extensively remodeled. Thus, Schindler resides eternally and ethereally in the house he designed and in which he lived.

Norman SCHLOSSMAN
(1901-1990)

Zion Gardens Cemetery,
Chicago, Illinois

ARCHITECTS' GRAVESITES | 91

Schlossman was a founding partner in the firm of Loebl Schlossman, which built several buildings in and around Chicago. He is buried within the Schlossman family plot, which is noted with a granite marker.

Richard SCHMIDT
(1865-1959)

Rosehill Cemetery, Chicago, Illinois

Schmidt practiced architecture in Chicago in the firm of Schmidt, Garden & Erickson. The Schmidt site bears an upright granite marker encircled with bands of weathered bronze that incorporate the family name. It is likely that Hugh Garden, Schmidt's architect partner, designed this monument. A headstone for Schmidt lies in front of the marker.

Paul SCHWEIKHER
(1903-1997)

Schaumburg, Illinois

Born in Denver, Colorado, Schweikher studied architecture at the Art Institute of Chicago, the Armour Institute (later the Illinois Institute of Technology), and Yale University. During his career, he worked with architects David Adler, George Keck, and Philip Maher. He went on to head the schools of architecture at Yale University and Carnegie University. He gained prominence by being part of the famous exhibit on modern architecture at the Museum of Modern Art in New York in 1932.

Despite his significant career in architecture, relatively few buildings are credited to him. One of the most significant of those is his own home and studio. It therefore seems fitting that it is in the backyard of this home that his ashes were scattered.

Josep Luis SERT
(1902-1983)

Cemetery of the Church of Jesus, Ibiza, Spain

 AIA Gold Medal 1981

While not American, Sert had significant impact on this country's mid-century architectural design evolution. He studied architecture in Barcelona and trained with Le Corbusier in France. He designed the Spanish pavilion in Paris in 1937, where Picasso's *Guernica* mural was first shown. He then moved to the United States to become dean of the Graduate School of Design at Harvard University. While in this country he designed the Holyoke Center and the Peabody Terrace and Science Center, both at Harvard. He also designed buildings for Boston University. He became a U.S. citizen in 1951 and brought in Le Corbusier to design the Carpenter Center at Harvard in 1965.

After his time in Cambridge, Sert returned to Barcelona, and it was there that he died. His ashes, along with his wife's, are located in a recess of a cemetery wall that is part of an ancient church on a Spanish island, an area that Sert loved and where he had a home. The thoughtful placement of the grave tablets suggest that Sert, himself, had a large role in the design of his gravesite.

Robert Edward SEYFARTH
(1878-1950)

Oakwood Cemetery,
Genesco, Illinois

After completing trade school, Seyfarth went to work for George Washington Maher, a prominent residential architect in the Chicago area. He worked on many of Maher's projects before starting his own practice in 1909. His revivalism broke away from the Prairie Style of his mentor Maher. His designs emphasized strong geometric shapes, carefully developed proportions, and elegant details based on historical references. His early projects were in his hometown of Blue Island, Illinois, but he soon settled in Highland Park, Illinois. It was there that he built a house for himself that received considerable attention, leading to several residential commissions along the North Shore of Chicago.

Ironically, his house was directly across the street from the Ward Willits House, designed by Frank Lloyd Wright. It seems that by driving down that street prospective clients could choose between the futuristic look of the Ward Willits House and the more traditional Seyfarth House.

Seyfarth's stone marker notes simply the names and dates of both him and his wife.

Alfred SHAW
(1895-1970)

Graceland Cemetery,
Chicago, Illinois

Shaw was a designer for the firm of Graham, Anderson, Probst & White and was responsible for the designs of the Civic Opera House and the Merchandise Mart in Chicago. His grave is marked with a modest headstone.

Howard Van Doren SHAW
(1869-1926)

Graceland Cemetery,
Chicago, Illinois

✽ AIA Gold Medal 1927

George Foster SHEPLEY
(1860-1903)

Walnut Hills Cemetery,
Brookline, Massachusetts

Shaw had a long career designing homes for the wealthy in Chicago's suburbs. Leonard Eaton wrote a book in which he compared Shaw's more conservative clients with the more adventuresome ones of his contemporary, Frank Lloyd Wright.

Shaw's gravesite is marked with a pylon upon which is perched a bronze globe that has the twenty-third psalm inscribed on it. It is believed that Shaw himself designed this monument.

Shepley was a partner in the firm of Shepley, Rutan & Coolidge, which continued the office of H. H. Richardson after Richardson's death. Shepley, a son-in-law of H. H. Richardson, is buried in the Richardson plot, along with his wife, Richardson's daughter Julia. His gravesite is marked with an ornate ledger that is of the same style of that of his father-in-law, whose grave is nearby. The inscription on the marker includes both Shepley and his wife.

Joseph L. SILSBEE
(1848-1913)

Oakwood Cemetery,
Syracuse, New York

Louis SKIDMORE
(1897-1962)

Lakeside Memorial Park,
Winter Haven, Florida

 AIA Gold Medal 1957

Silsbee was an acclaimed residential architect who employed several architects later famous in their own right, such as Frank Lloyd Wright, George Elmslie, and George Washington Maher. His grave is located on a gentle hillside and is marked with a small rough-hewn piece of red granite. On the marker are his name and that of his wife, Anna. The stone also includes the curious inscription: "In some brighter clime bid me good morning."

Skidmore, a founding partner in the firm of Skidmore, Owings & Merrill, was also the brother-in-law of Nathaniel Owings, another founding partner of SOM.

His simple grave personifies what had been Skidmore's quiet, understated demeanor. The standard military marker describes only his military achievements, with no hint that this man had a hand in establishing one of the most important and prolific architectural firms of all time.

George Washington SNOW
(1797-1870)

Graceland Cemetery,
Chicago, Illinois

Paolo SOLERI
(1919-2013)

Arcosanti,
Phoenix, Arizona

Snow is credited with having developed the balloon frame for house construction, which transformed the home-building industry in the late nineteenth century. Rather than requiring large custom-fabricated units for construction, the balloon frame technique allowed the use of light, standard-sized lumber.

Snow's gravesite contains a large obelisk with his name shown on a side panel. His actual grave is marked with a modest headstone bearing only his initials.

Soleri was born in Italy and received a PhD in architecture before immigrating to the United States. After apprenticing with Frank Lloyd Wright he struck off on his own career. He developed a philosophy of combining architecture with ecology—"arology," as he called it, which promoted densely packed living as an alternative to urban sprawl. He put this concept into practice in a development he called Arcosanti. With his eccentric and charismatic personality he attracted many followers to his development in the desert outside Phoenix.

It was there that he died and was buried, next to his wife, on a hillside in his own private desert cemetery, which can be seen from his studio window. The two cast bronze markers for Soleri and his wife were designed by the staff at Arcosanti and incorporate shapes used in precast panels featured in Arcosanti buildings. The fact that they are mirror images of each other symbolizes their close partnership.

Raphael SORIANO
(1904-1988)

Home of Peace Memorial Park, Los Angeles, California

An architect and educator, Soriano helped define what became known as midcentury modern architecture. Practicing primarily in southern California, he was one of the first to use prefabricated aluminum and steel in his designs.

Sadly, Soriano's burial site bears only a temporary marker. His followers intend to replace this with a more permanent marker sometime in the future.

Clarence S. STEIN
(1882-1975)

Croton-on-the-Hudson, New York

 AIA Gold Medal 1956

While growing up in New York City, Stein was exposed to the progressive Ethical Culture movement, which espouses having a more fulfilled life by honoring ethical principles. In Stein's case this had a profound effect on his interest in providing better urban environments. He was schooled at the Ecole des Beaux-Arts and Columbia University and became an architect and urban planner. He and his architectural partner, Henry Wright, are known for several innovative urban-planning projects, including Sunnyside Gardens in New York City and Chatham Village in Pittsburgh.

It is believed that his ashes were scattered at his former country home in Croton-on-the-Hudson.

James F. STIRLING
(1926-1992)

Christ Church,
Spitalfields, London

Edward Durell STONE
(1902-1978)

Evergreen Cemetery,
Fayetteville, Arkansas

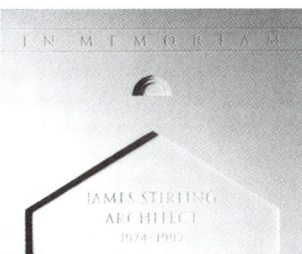

Though Stirling spent his entire life in Britain, he has been acknowledged as one of the important architects of the late twentieth century. He designed several university buildings in the United States, including the Sackler Museum at Harvard University and the School of Architecture at Rice University.

While never residing in the United States, Stirling designed several buildings at Harvard, Rice, and Cornell Universities that received considerable attention. What locks in his inclusion is the wonderful memorial plaque that was designed for him by his friend, sculptor Celia Scott, and executed by Lois Anderson. In her design she embodies elements of his design for the Clore entrance to the Tate Gallery into the stone marker at his gravesite. Stirling's ashes are contained in a small slate box designed by his wife that is buried beneath the stone floor.

Stone is known for his many designs that extend throughout the world, such as the Kennedy Center for the Performing Arts in Washington, D.C., and the United States Embassy in New Delhi, India.

His grave is within a Stone family plot on a gentle slope that overlooks the University of Arkansas, to which Stone always felt a close relationship. The simple graphics on his headstone mimic those of the family members around him, the only differentiation being the inscription "architect."

Oscar G. STONOROV
(1905-1970)

Phoenixville, Pennsylvania

Stonorov was born in Frankfurt, Germany, and studied in Florence, Italy, and Zurich, Switzerland. He apprenticed with sculptor Aristide Maillol in Paris and became an accomplished sculptor.

He came to the United States in 1929 and settled in Philadelphia, where he joined forces with Louis Kahn to design several housing projects, notably the Carl Mackley Housing, which is now on the National Register. He also compiled, in eight volumes, the archives of Le Corbusier.

Stonorov was killed in a plane crash that also took the life of his friend and patron, labor leader Walter Reuther. A family member has advised that his ashes were scattered on the grounds of his beloved home, Avon Lea Farm, which he created around an old stone farmhouse.

William STRICKLAND
(1788-1854)

Capitol Building, Nashville, Tennessee

Strickland was an early American architect who designed many neoclassical buildings. His career had entered something of a hiatus when he was chosen to design the new Tennessee State Capitol Building. He died during its construction, and the commissioners of the project determined that his remains should be part of what was perhaps his most important work. To be commemorated like a fallen prince within a great government building makes this a tribute of the highest order for an architect.

Hugh STUBBINS
(1912-2006)

Mt. Auburn Cemetery,
Cambridge, Massachusetts

Stubbins was born in Alabama. After receiving a degree from Georgia Institute of Technology he attended Harvard University, where he received a master's degree in architecture. He continued on at Harvard as a faculty member for several years.

Stubbins is perhaps best known for his Citigroup Building in New York City. His cremated remains reside behind a modest engraved plaque upon a mausoleum wall.

Louis Henri SULLIVAN
(1856-1924)

Graceland Cemetery,
Chicago, Illinois

 AIA Gold Medal 1944

Sullivan is considered by many to be the father of modern urban architecture and was one of the leaders of the great architectural movement that took place in the late nineteenth century in Chicago. Not only were the buildings that Sullivan designed important, but his writings and teachings also had a profound impact on those who followed him.

After successfully designing scores of buildings each year with his partner, Dankmar Adler, his practice fell off to only a handful of buildings in the last several years of his life. This was due to public infatuation with neoclassical architecture, which arose from the 1893 Columbian Exposition in Chicago, as well as his own difficult personality and addiction to alcohol. As a result, he died virtually penniless.

Not until twenty years after his death did the AIA acknowledge his importance with an award of the AIA Gold Medal. It also took several years for his friends and followers to mount a successful effort to provide a fitting monument for him. Leading the effort was architect Thomas Tallmadge, who came up with the design for Sullivan's monument—a rough-hewn granite block with skyscraper shapes emerging from both sides. On the back is an inscription commemorating Sullivan and his contributions. Behind the large marker is a modest headstone bearing Sullivan's name and dates. Alongside are the headstones of his mother and father.

It is ironic that literally casting a shadow on Sullivan's grave is the nearby Kimball monument. This large neoclassical edifice was designed by the prestigious firm of McKim, Mead & White. It was that highly influential firm and its promulgation of the neoclassical style that helped crush Sullivan's career.

Gene SUMMERS
(1928-2011)

San Francisco, California

Summers is best known for his close collaboration with Mies van der Rohe. He was essentially Mies's "right hand" on several major projects, including the Seagram Building in New York City. He left Mies's office in 1967 and went on to become chief of design at the Chicago firm of C. F. Murphy Associates, where he designed his most important work, the McCormick Place Exposition Center. Later on he went into real estate development and teaching.

Summers wanted no permanent marker for himself. His ashes were scattered in San Francisco Bay, near where he lived at the time of his death.

Thomas TALLMADGE
(1876-1940)

Graceland Cemetery,
Chicago, Illinois

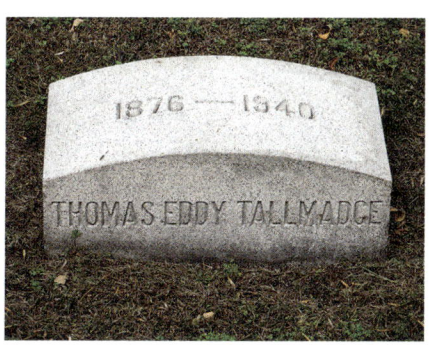

Tallmadge met Vernon Watson while both were working at the D. H. Burnham firm in Chicago. They left in 1905 and formed the firm of Tallmadge & Watson. They are known for the many residences and churches they designed in the Prairie Style. Tallmadge is buried with other family members, all having similar headstones. They lie within the family plot of the Eddys, Tallmadge's mother's family. The plot is marked with a large obelisk.

Robert Robertson TAYLOR
(1868-1942)

Pine Forest Cemetery,
Wilmington, North Carolina

Taylor was the first African American to graduate in architecture from the Massachusetts Institute of Technology. He was a friend and assistant to Booker T. Washington at Tuskegee Institute, where Taylor taught for several years and designed several of its buildings. He considered the chapel there to be his best work; later, ironically, he died, of a heart attack, in that building. The USPS issued a stamp in his honor in 1915. His simple marker gives the names and dates for him and his wife.

Benjamin C. THOMPSON
(1918-2002)

Mt. Auburn Cemetery,
Cambridge, Massachusetts

 AIA Gold Medal 1992

Thompson helped persuade Walter Gropius to form The Architects Collaborative (TAC) which, with its unique team approach, made it a leader after World War II.

Later Thompson, with his own firm, BTA, teamed up with developer James W. Rouse to create such notable people-oriented urban projects as Faneuil Hall Marketplace in Boston, Harborplace in Baltimore, and South Seaport in New York City. Critic Robert Campbell wrote of Thompson, "Probably no other architect of his time did more to change the face of America."

His remains lie beneath a boulder upon which are inscribed his name, dates, and the inscription: "Architect, Visionary, Naturalist."

William THORNTON
(1759-1828)

Congressional Cemetery,
Washington, D.C.

A licensed medical doctor as well as an architect, Thornton is known for the original design of the Capitol Building in Washington, D.C. Later additions were designed by Latrobe and Bulfinch. His burial site is memorialized with a large white stone marker set upon a ledger.

Ithiel TOWN
(1784-1844)

Grove Street Cemetery,
New Haven, Connecticut

Henry TROST
(1860-1933)

Evergreen Cemetery,
El Paso, Texas

Town was an early American architect. Among his works are two of the churches on the New Haven Green. He also invented the lattice truss bridge, now known as the Town Truss. His marker is a granite headstone with the symbols of his trade (T-square, triangle, and compass) as well as a description of his design accomplishments.

Trost designed hundreds of buildings in El Paso, Texas, and throughout the Southeast. Many of his buildings show a strong relationship to the designs of his former employer, Louis Sullivan. His burial site was originally marked only with a simple headstone. In subsequent years, a more formal monument was installed that includes a bronze tablet spelling out his many accomplishments.

Anne TYNG
(1920-2011)

Tyng was born in China while her New England parents, both Episcopalian missionaries, were serving there. She attended Radcliffe College and went on to the Harvard Graduate School of Design, where she was one of that school's first female graduates. In 1945 she went to work for Louis Kahn in Philadelphia, where her lifelong interest in geometric patterns evolved.

Over the next twenty-nine years, she developed a strong affiliation with Kahn, being credited for having had a significant hand in the design of several of his buildings, such as the Trenton Bath House and the Yale Art Gallery. She and Kahn also became romantically involved; she bore him a daughter while he was married to another woman. After Kahn's death she went on to teach morphology at the University of Pennsylvania, where she earned a PhD degree in 1975.

Tyng died at the age ninety-one. Her cremated remains are in the possession of a family member in Pennsylvania.

Richard UPJOHN
(1802-1878)

St. Philip's Church Cemetery, Garrison, New York

After moving to the United States from England, where he was born, Upjohn focused his design interests on the Gothic Style. Among his most famous buildings is Trinity Church in New York City. His work helped influence a wave of interest in the Gothic Style that spread throughout the country. Upjohn was a cofounder of the American Institute of Architects and was that organization's first president. He is buried beneath a stylized Celtic cross.

Richard UPJOHN, JR.
(1828-1903)

Green-Wood Cemetery,
Brooklyn, New York

Joseph URBAN
(1872-1933)

Sleepy Hollow Cemetery,
Sleepy Hollow, New York

Like his father, Richard Upjohn, Jr., specialized in the design of Gothic style churches. Also like his father, his gravesite is marked with a Celtic cross, the center panel of which displays his name.

Urban was an Austrian-born architect, illustrator, and set designer. He came to the United States in 1912 and became art director of the Boston Opera Company. He then moved to New York City, where he designed productions for the Ziegfeld Follies and the Metropolitan Opera. As an architect he is credited with being one of the originators of the art deco style.

Urban's remains lie beneath a black stone ledger with art deco lettering showing his name and dates.

William VAN ALEN
(1882-1954)

Cold Spring Cemetery,
Cold Spring, New York

Henry VAN BRUNT
(1832-1903)

Cambridge Cemetery,
Cambridge, Massachusetts

Van Alen is best known as the architect of the Chrysler Building in New York City. He in buried beneath a large granite headstone decorated with a small rosette and his name and dates. Next to it is a similar marker for his wife. Both stand in front of a large monument for the Van Alen family.

Born in Boston, Van Brunt attended Harvard University before teaming up with fellow architect William Ware to form the firm of Ware & Van Brunt. The firm designed many buildings, several of which are on the Harvard campus, including Memorial Hall. Van Brunt later formed a partnership with Frank Howe and their firm, Van Brunt & Howe, designed many buildings in the Richardsonian Romanesque style. Van Brunt is buried beneath a stone ledger listing him and other family members.

John VAN OSDEL
(1811-1891)

Rosehill Cemetery,
Chicago, Illinois

Van Osdel is considered to be Chicago's first architect. Many of his early buildings were destroyed in the Chicago fire of 1871. Van Osdel's modest headstone lies in front of a family marker.

Calvert VAUX
(1824-1895)

Montrepose Cemetery,
Kingston, New York

Vaux was a noted and well-established British-born landscape designer when he took on the relatively inexperienced Fredrick Law Olmsted as a partner in the development of Central Park in New York City. This was the project that catapulted Olmsted into prominence and was the beginning of his extraordinary career. Though Vaux went on to design many more projects, his name has never reached the level of acclaim afforded Olmsted.

Vaux's gravesite is defined by a large stone monolith that commemorates Vaux as well as his wife and daughter.

Konrad WACHSMANN
(1901-1980)

Friedhof Cemetery,
Frankfurt an der Oder, Germany

Wachsmann was a German-born architect known for his contributions to the mass production of buildings. He began as an apprentice to a cabinet maker and studied in arts and crafts schools in Berlin and Dresden. Along the way he designed a summer house for Albert Einstein, and the two became lifelong friends.

He moved to the United States in 1941 and collaborated with Walter Gropius on a packaged house system. He also designed several innovative aircraft hangars for the United States Air Force. He went on to teach for several years at the Illinois Institute of Technology in Chicago and at the University of Southern California in Los Angeles.

His marker is a smartly shaped stone slab with an elegant font that proclaims his name and his profession.

Ralph Thomas WALKER
(1889-1973)

Fair Lawn Cemetery,
Ridgefield, Connecticut

✺ AIA Gold Medal 1957—Centennial Award

Born in Connecticut, Walker attended the Massachusetts Institute of Technology but left before receiving a degree. After working in several architectural offices, Walker joined the firm of McKenzie, Voorhees & Gmelin, a firm for which he would work his entire career. In 1926, his art deco-style Barclay-Vesey Building in New York established him as a designer of note, and he became a partner in the firm that ultimately became Voorhees, Walker, Smith, Smith & Haines. He went on to design other significant buildings in New York and elsewhere, including several pavilions at the 1939 New York World's Fair.

Walker was a president of the American Institute of Architects, and in 1957 he received an AIA Centennial Medal of Honor, an award specially created for him. As a result, the *New York Times* identified him as "the Architect of the Century." However, Walker had a falling out with the AIA in 1959, when his firm was accused of behaving unprofessionally. In a fit of anger, Walker resigned and destroyed the medal he had received from that organization.

Walker took his own life in 1973 in what was possibly one of the most dramatic demises of any architect. It is rumored that Walker shot himself using a bullet he had forged out of gold from his AIA award.

The markers commemorating him and his wife lie beneath a stone exedra. Just a few feet away is the monument of fellow architect Cass Gilbert.

Walker was a mid-twentieth-century architect who designed many houses in southern California, including three for John Entenza's Case Study House Program. He graduated from the University of California at Los Angeles and received most of his architectural training as a draftsman working for Rudolph Schindler. He considered his masterpiece the large house he built for himself in Ojai, California.

After his death his ashes were deposited in the Pacific Ocean at Santa Barbara.

Thomas U. WALTER
(1804-1887)

Laurel Hill Cemetery,
Philadelphia, Pennsylvania

Rodney WALKER
(1910-1986)

Santa Barbara, California

Walter is possibly the foremost American architect between the death of Benjamin Latrobe in 1820 and the emergence of Richardson in the 1870s.

He is best known as the fourth architect of the U.S. Capitol Building and was responsible for the Senate and House wings of the building as well as the central cast-iron dome. He was a founding member of the American Institute of Architects and its second president.

His burial site is marked with a stone tablet and a bronze plate, added later, that describes his achievements.

William WARE
(1832-1915)

Mt. Auburn Cemetery, Cambridge, Massachusetts

Ware was an influential architect and educator, becoming the first professor of architecture at the Massachusetts Institute of Technology, the institution that offered the first formal course in architecture in the country. He went on to found the architecture department at Columbia University. His most notable work was Memorial Hall at Harvard, which he designed with Henry van Brunt.

His headstone is a simple slate slab stating his name, dates, and parentage.

John Carl WARNECKE
(1919-2010)

Healdsburg, California

112 | ARCHITECTS' GRAVESITES

Warnecke was a prolific architect, known especially for his designs for Lafayette Park in Washington, D.C., and the Kennedy Memorial in Arlington National Cemetery. At one time his firm, John Carl Warnecke & Associates, was the largest in the United States. Ironically, working for him were Eugene Kohn, William Pedersen, and Sheldon Fox who, in 1976, left to form their own firm. Today Kohn Pedersen Fox Associates (KPF) is one of the largest architectural firms in the world.

Warnecke spent most of his time in California, eventually retiring to his vineyard estate in Healdsburg. It was there that he died at the age of ninety-one. He asked that a portion of his ashes be scattered beneath a favorite live oak tree on his cherished estate. That site is marked with a bronze plaque affixed to a granite boulder. At a future date the rest of his ashes are to be interred at Mountain View Cemetery, Oakland, California.

Vernon WATSON
(1878-1950)

Rosehill Cemetery,
Chicago, Illinois

Watson was a partner with Thomas Talmadge. His remains are buried in the Watson family plot. While there are markers for his wife, his brother, and his mother, there is no marker for Vernon Watson.

Harry WEESE
(1915-1998)

Lake Michigan

Weese was known as a highly independent and imaginative architect. Educated at the Massachusetts Institute of Technology and Yale University, Weese joined the Cranbrook Academy and developed a close relationship with Eero Saarinen. This relationship helped introduce Weese to the burgeoning architecture program in Columbus, Indiana, where Weese was selected to design several buildings early in his career. Weese established his office in Chicago and went on to design several office towers and residences, and as well as stations for the Washington, D.C., Metro system.

His love of sailing was the basis for his wish that his ashes be scattered on his beloved Lake Michigan.

Otis WHEELOCK
(1816-1893)

Graceland Cemetery,
Chicago, Illinois

Wheelock was a prolific architect, having at one time offices in several major cities, including Chicago. Despite Wheelock's successful practice there, he detested the city and its roughness. It is therefore ironic that his final resting place is in the city he so disliked. He was buried in his family's plot in Chicago, marked with a large obelisk. A simple headstone marks his grave.

Howard Judson WHITE
(1870-1936)

Graceland Cemetery,
Chicago, Illinois

White was a partner in the firm of Graham, Anderson, Probst & White. When Ernest Graham, the senior partner in the firm, died in 1936, the firm was quickly restructured, literally putting Graham's secretary, C. F. Murphy, out on the street. Murphy set about establishing his own firm and went after some of the clients of the GAP&W firm. After learning at a meeting with Field Enterprises, one of his firm's oldest and most valued clients, that they were switching their business to the new Murphy firm, White suffered a heart attack and died on the way back to his office.

White's grave is marked with an unadorned headstone, similar to that of his wife, who is buried beside him.

Stanford WHITE
(1853-1906)

St. James Episcopal Church Graveyard,
St. James, New York

White was a bigger-than-life personality and a partner in the firm of McKim, Mead & White. His end came when he was shot by a jealous husband who believed that White was involved with his wife. The murder occurred in the tower of the old Madison Square Garden Building, one of White's designs.

At his burial site is a tall granite marker, softened with delicate ornamentation, that notes both Stanford White and his wife, Bessie, who lived until 1950.

Philip WILL
(1906-1985)

Higgins Lake, Michigan

Will was a founding partner with Lawrence Perkins of the firm of Perkins & Will, designers of office buildings and schools throughout the country. Will, a native of Rochester, New York, attended Cornell University, where he and Perkins became acquainted as roommates. After college Will worked for several years at the New York firm of Shreve, Lamb & Harmon. In 1934, Will and his wife, on their honeymoon, traveled to Chicago to see the Century of Progress exposition. It was there that Perkins, who had been Will's best man, persuaded Will to stay in Chicago and join him working for a local architectural firm, General Houses, Inc. In 1935, the two architects struck out on their own and, along with another colleague, Todd Wheeler, formed the firm of Perkins, Wheeler & Will. Shortly thereafter, their firm was catapulted into national exposure by their design for the Crow Island School in Winnetka, Illinois. Created in collaboration with Eliel Saarinen, the school's design broke away from traditional thinking, with its single story, independent classrooms allowing outside access, and child-scaled dimensions and details. This project propelled the firm, which eventually became Perkins & Will, into perhaps the leading designers of schools throughout the country. The firm went on to design important office buildings as well, including the U.S. Gypsum Building and the Standard Oil Building (in collaboration with Edward Durell Stone), both in Chicago.

Will died in Florida and his ashes were scattered over Higgins Lake, Michigan, the site of his family's vacation home.

Paul R. WILLIAMS
(1894-1980)

Manchester Garden Mausoleum, Inglewood Park Cemetery, Inglewood, California

❀ AIA Gold Medal 1947

Williams is best known for the houses he designed in the Los Angeles area. He was master of several styles and designed over 2,000 dwellings, including ones for celebrities Frank Sinatra, Lucille Ball, Tyrone Power, Lon Chaney, Bert Lahr, and Barbara Stanwyck. He also designed Al Jolson's tomb.

He was the first African American to become a Fellow of the AIA. In 2017, he was awarded the AIA Gold Medal posthumously. A large memorial to him was constructed next to the Golden State Mutual Life Insurance Building in Los Angeles, a building that he designed.

His remains reside in a mausoleum crypt marked for him and his wife with metal lettering.

Lebbeus WOODS
(1940-2012)

Woods was a most unconventional and visionary architect. While he actually built nothing, he made a significant impact with his teachings, writings, and, above all, his drawings, which have been compared to Piranesi and Escher.

Woods requested no burial, so his ashes are in the possession of a family member.

Frank Lloyd WRIGHT
(1867-1959)

Spring Green, Wisconsin

Taliesin,
Scottsdale, Arizona

❀ AIA Gold Medal 1949

Wright had a long, productive, and controversial life. Many books have been written describing this extraordinarily important, multifaceted, creative, and self-promoting genius. To highlight his prominence, in 1966 the USPS issued a commemorative stamp in his honor.

When Wright died, his body was buried in a small churchyard at the base of his home at Taliesin in Wisconsin. There he joined the remains of his mother and of his mistress, Mamah Cheney, and her two children, who died in a tragic fire at Taliesin. A lovely monument was constructed that consisted of an art glass panel with his name and the inscription: "Love of an idea is love of God." Next to this was a large boulder resting on edge. Embedded stones outlined his burial site and the entire ensemble was contained within a great circle of sunken stones.

Wright's third wife, Olgivanna, stipulated that after her death, Wright's remains be disinterred, cremated, moved to Arizona, and mixed with her ashes. Unbeknownst to local Wisconsin authorities, her wishes were carried out; Wright's remains were removed, literally in the dead of night, and sent to California. There are still hard feelings about the way the remains of one of Wisconsin's famous sons were "stolen." Thus, the Frank Lloyd Wright Memorial Foundation is unwilling to disclose where the comingled ashes were placed at Taliesin West. A portion of these ashes was reportedly cast upon the Arizona desert as well.

Wright had progeny with distinguished architectural careers of their own. His son Lloyd Wright (1890-1978) designed the famous Wayfayers Chapel in Palos Verdes, California. His son John Lloyd Wright (1892-1972), besides his architectural work, created Lincoln Logs for children. Granddaughter Elizabeth Wright Ingraham (1922-2013) also designed several projects. The ashes of Lloyd were scattered at his favorite property high in Santa Monica, California overlooking the Pacific. John's were scattered in the ocean in front of his house in Del Mar, California. Those of his granddaughter were taken to sites in Colorado and the family cemetery in Spring Green, California.

William WURSTER
(1894-1973)

 AIA Gold Medal 1969

Being brought up in the Bay Area, Wurster followed the Mission Style design tradition of Bernard Maybeck in the many houses he designed. He is best known, however, as an educator, having been dean of architecture at both the Massachusetts Institute of Technology and the University of California at Berkeley, where the school's architecture building is named for him.

His wife, Catherine Bauer Wurster (1905-1964), is best known as an authority on public housing. Her 1934 book *Modern Housing* is considered a classic on the subject, and her advice was important in shaping early public housing policies. She died prematurely in a hiking accident on Mount Tamalpais in Marin County, California. A family member says that the ashes of both the Wursters were scattered at a Bay Area cemetery, possibly Mountain View Cemetery in Oakland, where the remains of Julia Morgan and Bernard Maybeck reside.

Minoru YAMASAKI
(1912-1966)

Lakeville Cemetery,
Lakeville, Michigan

Yamasaki is known for the several large projects he designed, including the Lambert-St. Louis International Airport terminal and the McGregor Memorial Conference Center in Detroit, Michigan. Perhaps his crowning achievements were the World Trade Center twin towers in New York City, which were destroyed on September 11, 2001.

A second-generation Japanese American, he attended schools in Washington before moving to New York City in the 1930s to join the firm of Shreve, Lamb & Harmon, designers of the Empire State Building. His employer helped him prevent his parents, still living in Seattle, from being interned during World War II. After the war he moved to Detroit, where he eventually established his own firm, Yamasaki & Associates, in 1949.

His style rejected the starkness of the modernist movement. Instead he moved toward incorporating decorative motifs in his designs. It was for this that he received mounting criticism. The well-publicized destruction of his Pruitt Igoe Housing Project in St. Louis in 1972 was a further blow to his reputation. Nevertheless, this modest, unpretentious man was asked to design what would become a symbol of American greatness in the 1970s, the World Trade Center twin towers.

Yamasaki's cremated remains are buried, along with his wife's, in a remote country cemetery. This serene and gracious setting is perhaps the finest of any architect's final resting place. This site was selected by a family member who lives nearby. Yamasaki lies beneath a towering pine tree, his gravesite marked by two substantial boulders. These boulders were so treasured by Yamasaki that he had them moved along with his family as they relocated to various homes. The origin of the boulders is unknown. In front of one is a simple marker giving the names and dates of Yamasaki and his wife. Etched faintly beneath the two names is the image of a lotus flower, a symbol of rebirth. The second boulder, lying next to the base of the pine tree, is intended as a place of repose for family while visiting the grave.

GEOGRAPHICAL GROUPINGS

UNITED STATES

ARIZONA

Phoenix	Arcosanti	Paolo Soleri
	National Memorial Cemetery	Alfred N. Beadle
Scottsdale	Taliesin	Frank Lloyd Wright

ARKANSAS

Eureka Springs	Thorncrown Chapel	E. Fay Jones
Fayetteville	Evergreen Cemetery	Edward Durell Stone

CALIFORNIA

Big Sur	Wild Bird	Nathaniel Owings
Healdsburg		John Carl Warnecke
Hollywood	Westwood Cemetery	Franklin D. Israel
Inglewood	Ingelwood Park Cemetery	Paul R. Williams
Los Angeles	Home of Peace Memorial Park	Raphael Soriano
	Los Angeles National Cemetery	Pierre Koenig
Monterey	Cemetario el Encinal	Charles Willard Moore
	Monterey Cemetery	Charles Sumner Greene
Ojai		Julius-Ralph Davidson
Palm Springs	Welwood Murray Cemetery	Albert Frey
Piedmont	Mountain View Cemetery	Bernard Maybeck
		Julia Morgan
Port Richmond		Gerald A. Horn
San Gabriel	San Gabriel Cemetery	Henry Mather Greene
		Myron Hunt
Silver Lake	Neutra House	Richard Neutra
West Hollywood	Schindler House	Rudolph Schindler

COLORADO

Denver	Logan National Cemetery	Jacques Brownson

CONNECTICUT

Farmington	Riverside Cemetery	Theodate Pope Riddle
Hamden	Central Burying Grounds	John Gerard Dinkeloo
Hartford	Old North Cemetery	Fredrick Law Olmsted
		Frederick Law Olmsted, Jr.
New Canaan	Glass House Rose Garden	Philip Johnson
New Haven	Grove Street Cemetery	Henry Austin
		Ithiel Town
Ridgefield	Fairlawn Cemetery	Cass Gilbert
		Ralph Thomas Walker
South Manchester	Cheney Family Plot	Charles Platt

DISTRICT OF COLUMBIA

Washington	Congressional Cemetery	Robert Mills
		William Thornton
	Mt. Olivet Cemetery	James Hoban

FLORIDA

Miami	Lakeside Memorial Park	Morris Lapidus
Tequesta	Riverside Memorial Cemetery	Bruce Graham
Winter Haven	Lakeside Memorial Park	Louis Skidmore

ILLINOIS

Barrington	St. Michael's Episcopal Church	Edward Dart
Chicago	Graceland Cemetery	David Adler
		Peirce Anderson
		Augustus Bauer
		Jacques Brownson*
		Daniel Hudson Burnham
		George Grant Elmslie
		Stanislaw Gladych*
		Bruce Goff
		Bruce Graham*
		Ernest Graham
		John Augur Holabird
		John Augur Holabird, Jr.
		William Holabird
		William Le Baron Jenney
		Fazlur Khan
		Gertrude Lempp Kerbis
		Marion Mahony (Griffin)
		Ludwig Mies van der Rohe
		László Moholy-Nagy
		Walter Netsch
		Dwight Perkins
		Lawrence Perkins
		John Wellborn Root
		John Wellborn Root, Jr.
		Alfred Shaw
		Howard Van Doren Shaw
		George Washington Snow
		Louis Henri Sullivan
		Thomas Tallmadge
		Otis Wheelock
		Howard Judson White

	Illinois Institute of Technology	Gerald A. Horn
	Mt. Mayriv Cemetery	Dankmar Adler
	Oak Woods Cemetery	Solon Beman
	Rosehill Cemetery	William W. Boyington
		Charles Frost
		Alfred Granger
		Jerrold Loebl
		George Washington Maher
		Philip Brooks Maher
		Benjamin Marshall
		Richard Schmidt
		John Van Osdel
		Vernon Watson
	Wunder's Cemetery	Frederick Dinkelberg
	Zion Gardens Cemetery	Norman Schlossman
Evanston	Calvary Cemetery	Barry Byrne
		Charles F. Murphy, Sr.
		Martin Roche
Evergreen park	St. Mary Cemetery	John W. Moutoussamy
Forest Park	Forest Home Cemetery	William Drummond
	Waldheim Cemetery	William Gray Purcell
Genesco	Oakwood Cemetery	Robert Edward Seyfarth
Lake Forest	Lake Forest Cemetery	Edward Bennett
		Edward Bennett, Jr.
Schaumburg	Schweikher House	Paul Schweikher
Skokie	Memorial Park	Myron Goldsmith
		Jens Jensen

KENTUCKY

Louisville	Cave Hill Cemetery	Stratton Hammon

LOUISIANA

New Orleans	St. Louis Cemetery No. 1	Benjamin Latrobe

MAINE

Castine	Castine Town Cemetery	William Hartmann
Mount Desert	Brookside Cemetery	Edward Larrabee Barnes

MARYLAND

Landover	National Harmony Memorial Park	Hilyard Robinson

MASSACHUSETTS

Brookline	Walnut Hills Cemetery	Henry Hobson Richardson
		Charles Rutan
		George Foster Shepley
Cambridge	Cambridge Cemetery	John Mead Howells
		Henry Van Brunt
	Mt. Auburn Cemetery	Asher Benjamin
		Richard Bennett
		Charles Bulfinch
		Charles Allerton Coolidge
		Henry Atherton Frost
		Buckminster Fuller
		George Howe
		Carl Koch
		Robert S. Peabody
		Eleanor Raymond
		Arthur Rotch
		Hugh Stubbins
		Benjamin C. Thompson
		William Ware
Martha's Vineyard	Chilmark Cemetery	Eliot F. Noyes
Millbury	Millbury Central Cemetery	Charles Bowler Atwood
Sudbury	St. Elizabeth's Church Chapel	Ralph Adams Cram
Wellfleet	Breuer House	Marcel Breuer

MICHIGAN

Ann Arbor	Forest Hill Cemetery	Allen Pond
		Irving Pond
Lakeville	Lakeville Cemetery	Minoru Yamasaki
Marquette	Midgaard	John Lautner
Midland	Midland Cemetery	Alden Dow
Troy	White Chapel Memorial Cemetery	Albert Kahn
		Eero Saarinen

MINNESOTA

Minneapolis	Lakewood Cemetery	Leroy Buffington
		Ralph Rapson

MISSISSIPPI

Meridan	Magnolia Cemetery	Samuel N. Mockbee

MISSOURI

St. Louis	Bellefontaine Cemetery	George Barnett
		James Eads
	Calvary Cemetery	Charles Eames
		Ray Eames

NEW JERSEY

Orange	Rosedale Cemetery	Charles McKim
Princeton	Princeton Cemetery	Michael Graves
Trenton	Riverview Cemetery	John Roebling

NEW MEXICO

Santa Fe	Franzen House	Ulrich Franzen

NEW YORK

Bronx	Woodlawn Cemetery	George Post
Brooklyn	Green-Wood Cemetery	James Bogardus
		Henry Ives Cobb
		James Renwick
		Richard Upjohn, Jr.
Buffalo	Forest Lawn Cemetery	Louise Bethune
	Temple Beth El	Gordon Bunshaft
Cold Spring	Cold Spring Cemetery	Washington Roebling
		William Van Alen
East Hampton	Green River Cemetery	Charles Gwathmey
Garrison	St. Philip's Church Cemetery	Richard Upjohn
Kingston	Montrepose Cemetery	Calvert Vaux
Manhattan	Church of the Intercession	Bertram Goodhue
Nassau County	St. John's Memorial Cemetery	William Adams Delano
St. James	St. James Episcopal Church	Stanford White
Sleepy Hollow	Sleepy Hollow Cemetery	Wallace Harrison
		Raymond Hood
		Joseph Urban

Syracuse	Oakwood Cemetery	Joseph L. Silsbee
	St. Agnes Cemetery	Harvey Ellis
Valhalla	Kensico Cemetery	William E. Lescaze
Yonkers	Oakland Cemetery	John Q. Hejduk

NORTH CAROLINA

Wilmington	Oakdale Cemetery	Henry Bacon
	Pine Forest Cemetery	Robert Robertson Taylor

PENNSYLVANIA

Chester Springs	St. Peter Pikeland Church	Vincent George Kling
Collingsdale	Eden Cemetery	Julian Francis Abele
Philadelphia		Henry S. Churchill
	Laurel Hill Cemetery	Frank Furness
		Thomas U. Walter
	Woodlands Cemetery	Paul Cret
Phoenixville		Edmund Bacon
Rockledge	Montefiore Cemetery	Louis Isidore Kahn

RHODE ISLAND

Middletown	Berkeley Memorial Cemetery	John Russell Pope
Newport	Island Cemetery	Richard Morris Hunt

TENNESSEE

Nashville	Tennessee State Capitol	William Strickland

TEXAS

El Paso	Evergreen Cemetery	Henry Trost

VERMONT

Charlotte		Dan Kiley

VIRGINIA

Arlington	Arlington National Cemetery	Pierre L'Enfant
		Montgomery Meigs
Charlottesville	Monticello Historic Site	Thomas Jefferson

WASHINGTON

Seattle	Evergreen Washelli Memorial Park	Welton David Becket

WISCONSIN

Bristol		Alfred Caldwell
Spring Green	Taliesin	Frank Lloyd Wright*
Watertown	Oak Hill Cemetery	George Fred Keck

(* indicates cenotaph)

INTERNATIONAL

ARGENTINA	Buenos Aires	Eduardo Catalano
AUSTRIA	Vienna	Victor Gruen
EGYPT	Cairo	Matthew (Maciej) Nowicki
ENGLAND	London	Zaha Hadid
	Spitalsfield	James F. Stirling
FINLAND	Helsinki	Alvar Aalto
	Kirkkonummi	Eliel Saarinen
FRANCE	**Cap Martin**, Roqubrune	Le Corbusier
GERMANY	Frankfurt an der Oder	Konrad Wachsmann
	Stahnsdorf	Walter Gropius
INDIA	Lucknow	Walter Burley Griffin
ITALY		Chester Holmes Aldrich
		Craig Ellwood
MEXICO	Mazunte	Raimund Abraham
	Mexico City	Ricardo Legorreta
POLAND	Warsaw	Stanislaw Gladych
		Matthew (Maciej) Nowicki*
SPAIN	Ibiza	Josep Luis Sert

(* indicates cenotaph)

AFTERWORD

To come to the end of this book is to conclude a journey across the United States, across architectural history, and into human character. I am not sure that the final resting places of celebrated and accomplished architects tell us all that much about their work—after all, few of them designed their own burial sites or grave markers, and the graves that most closely resemble the architecture of their occupants were quite often designed by others, sometimes many years later, and some have the forced quality of all-too-earnest homage.

But if the design of architects' gravesites sheds only minimal light on their work, their graves do tell us rather more than we might have expected about these architects as people. Some of them are grand and imposing, others so modest as to be no more than small stone plaques set flat upon the ground. Many architects chose to be buried with their families, and their grave markers confer equal billing to spouses and sometimes other family members. The extraordinary Julia Morgan shares her marker with nine of her relatives, and there is nary a mention of her noble career; Charles McKim's is somewhat grander and identifies him as "Architect," but says no more than that, and he, too, shares equal billing with his family.

Clearly the instinct toward modesty arises more often for architects in death than it does in life, since it is hard not to be surprised at how many of these final resting places are small and understated. A successful architect, after all, need not fear that he or she leaves nothing behind: the smallest building is usually larger than the most elaborate grave, and most of these architects have left plenty of buildings, most of which are not at all small, for us to remember them by.

Is a sense that their work is their memorial the reason a surprising number of architects have chosen to have no gravesites at all? Many asked to be cremated and to have their ashes scattered. And many of these have asked that their remains be cast upon the water—Lake Michigan (Harry Weese and Natalie de Blois), San Francisco Bay (Erich Mendelsohn and Gene Summers), Santa Monica Bay (William Pereira), the Atlantic Ocean (Serge Chermayeff) and the Pacific Ocean (Gregory Ain and Joseph Esherick). That so many people who spent their professional lives creating structures on land that would outlast them would choose to have their own remains scattered on the water is one of the ironic truths to be learned from *Architects' Gravesites*. Did they feel that their work constituted memorial enough on the land? Did they seek closeness to nature, after a lifetime of crafting the world of the man-made? Or did they perhaps fear that the physical form of a gravestone might in some way be viewed as a weak echo of their work?

Of course, what most of us want—what most of us turn the pages of *Architects' Gravesites* hoping to find—is some kind of echo of the architect's voice, however much many of the architects themselves shied away from expressing it. Those who allowed their gravesites to give a hint of their architecture bring the reader a particular pleasure: Michael Graves, for example, whose burial site is decorated with a postmodern structure that is utterly Gravesian, and Ralph Rapson, whose black stone marker, his name writ large, reflects the brutalist style of his work and with its cantilevered mass positively proclaims that an architect is buried beneath it. So, too, with Alden Dow, whose colleague Bill Gilmore designed what looks like an abstract rendition of an Alden Dow house in granite to mark his burial site. If these can seem a bit too self-conscious, they have the allure of all miniatures. It is impossible not to like them. And then there is Louis Sullivan, whose grave at Graceland Cemetery in Chicago—which contains the graves or memorials of more prominent architects than any other single place—is at once utterly Sullivanesque and boldly different. It consists of a rough-hewn block of granite with a medallion of Sullivan-like ornament on the front and carvings on the sides subtly evoking the lines of the skyscraper aesthetic Sullivan did so much to inspire. If the medallion evokes his style literally, the rough granite is a metaphor for his determined and obstinate character. (Sullivan, who died penniless, played no role in the design of his memorial; it was added to his gravesite years later by friends.)

A handful of architects avoided all ambiguity by being buried within buildings of their own design, thus assuring that we would follow the famous inscription over the monument to Sir Christopher Wren in St. Paul's Cathedral: "Si monumentum requiris, circumspice." If you seek the monument to Fay Jones, look about the Thorncrown Chapel; if you seek to honor Bertram Goodhue, look about the Chapel of the Intercession in upper Manhattan, although one can also look upon Goodhue himself, since he lies atop a catafalque sculpted with his likeness by his frequent collaborator, the sculptor Lee Lawrie. It is an oddly grandiose, not to say rather more traditional, memorial than one might expect for an architect who was not known for arrogance or for an unwillingness to push design in new directions. Goodhue's memorial is, if nothing else, an exception to the general premise that these resting places enlighten us to the nature of their character. More pleasing, surely, not to say more witty, was another burial within a house of worship: James Stirling, the British architect, who is honored by a plaque, its design inspired by his work, within Nicholas Hawksmoor's incomparable Christ Church Spitalfields, in London. Is this the ultimate act of modesty, deferring in death to the greatness of a predecessor? Or did Stirling want to tell us that he considered himself Hawksmoor's equal? We will never know for sure.

But all of these places, whether they intentionally evoke the rest of an architect's work or not, hold the power, like all burial sites, to transport us out of the moment. The sparseness of Mies van der Rohe's granite slab at Graceland, designed by his grandson Dirk Lohan, conveys Mies's aura more powerfully, surely, than anything more literally resembling his work could do, and the same could be said of so many others here. The form of these graves only begins to give significance to them. Their true meaning, in the end, comes from what we know of these architects and their work, the spirit of which lives on.

Paul Goldberger

Joseph Urban Professor of Design and Architecture
Parsons School of Design/
The New School
New York

contributing editor
Vanity Fair

former architectural critic
The New Yorker